14 ST...

2 WHEELS

AND 1 PAIR OF PANTS

CW00516744

Dearest Annabel,

Thank you for all your
support and love in life!

I adore You ♡
Gemma

A One Woman Cycle XXX
Across the USA

GEMMA STILWELL

DEDICATION

To My Whatsapp Peloton

For Your Love and Support

▍CONTENTS

| PROLOGUE

O n deciding to tell people that I was going to cycle across the USA in the Summer of 2019, people's reactions tended to fit into one of these two categories. Either something along the lines of 'why would you do that?', (or preferably) 'amazing!'. I enjoyed guessing which reaction it would be, and had my convincing spiel at the ready. I was determined to turn the 'why' reaction into being convinced by my masterful planning and my 'all will be well' attitude. In reality this never went that well and I spent most of my time convincing them I wasn't going to be eaten by a bear, run over by a truck, shot, get lost or some other comedic demise. I mean I had no idea what was going to happen, and why would I even want to? That's surely the whole point of the adventure, right?

I was so excited I could hardly contain it! I was going to cycle the 3300 or so miles solo from Seattle (on the west coast) to Washington D.C (on the east) in 6 weeks. The challenge was set and that was all anyone needed to know for now, the details would be figured out along the way.

So here it is, the story of my adventure, all the whys, wheres, whats, whos and hows in a round-a-bout order. I hope it to be a true and accurate account of life on the road, the 'eat, sleep, cycle, repeat', mixed with stories of the kindness of strangers, crazy 'only in America' happenings, and the amazing diverse mix of cultures and landscapes of this vast country. I hope this book is entertaining, somewhat educational and also a source of practical information for anyone wanting to plan their own adventures, female, solo, young, old or otherwise. Even if it only inspires one person to get on their bike or go and plan an adventure, I will be a very happy girl!

So let's begin…

PART
1
ALL IN THE PLANNING

WHY?

Wind back about 7 years previous, whilst on a trip to Center Parcs (might need to be in inverted commas?) with a whole bunch of my friends and their small people. One night (and to cut a long story short) two of us were required to go on a middle of the night random rescue mission out of the park and across the county to the 'nearest' hospital. Now, if any of you have ever been to Center Parcs, you will know how long it takes to escape these places. There was a lot of time to think and chat about my cycling dreams whilst passing the time in the middle of the night. Now I'm only telling you all this as it is my first memory of actually talking about cycling across the USA to a person rather than just in my head. After this time, it seemed too far and too big to achieve that I didn't mention it for years, however the seed was now planted. Whenever there has been a 'could I' possibility in my head, it's really really hard to get it to go away.

This idea did not spring up from nowhere, as my love of adventures had started way back with a 10 month back packing trip around the world after graduating. I experienced life as I could only imagine before, igniting something of a wanderlust in me that is ever present. As much as I love travel and think being an innately 'nomadic' person happy to set off on a whim would be brill, this is just not me. I also love my friends, my home, my career, and my future choices. Maybe if I didn't have this life to come back to, I would travel forever, but I do love coming home as much as I love going. It's all getting a bit deep now, but I hope you catch my drift that I seem to live somewhere between always wanting more, whilst perfectly content at the same time.

I'm lucky enough to have built a career as a freelance instrumental music teacher, aligning my 'working time' to the UK school term timetable. When schools are in I max out the work, then enjoy the extended holiday times as much as possible. I often think about new less lonely and more stable opportunities, but if it doesn't come with extended time off and a bit of flexibility it just doesn't make the cut. I think, in reality, only wild horses could drag me back to working for someone else, assuming anyone would employ this rogue in the first place!

Therefore, every year since returning from my world trip I have embarked on a summer adventure, a few of which were twinned with my life-long love of cycling. I make a policy of only taking the car if there is no cycling option, (or it's bucketing it down with rain), and always take pleasure in hiding a cheeky 'sorry not sorry' smile whilst whizzing my way through traffic jams!

My first cycle tour was in 2008 when I convinced a friend that we wanted to ride the thousand miles from 'Land's End to John O Groats' carrying all our stuff. This came about after I returned from my world trip, embarrassingly realising I have never gone further north than Manchester in my own country! We completed this trip in 3 weeks, averaging approximately 55 miles a day, albeit in the 'wrong' direction starting in Scotland. This was mainly for logistical reasons plus a general lack of planning about the importance of the prevailing winds! Novice error duly noted. This set the next plan in motion of cycling the 1300 miles from London to Rome in 2010, followed by a cycle from Budapest to Dubrovnik passing through six Capital cities in a completely random order in 2015. Unlike the first two trips we were not raising money for charity along the way with this one. We were now more 'experienced' and it looked like the easiest trip so far, with a slightly cheating sneaky train ride to save time. Amazing though it was, it was also arguably the hardest yet, and I learnt a lot more about taking elevation and road conditions into account and not just the mileage. Another important factor is the weather, which was a hard lesson learnt during a 2017 cycle around half of Ireland. A holiday I regularly forget even happened! If the very friendly people were anything to go by, I'm sure Ireland is as wonderful place. However, with only one day where it didn't constantly pour down, my hate of cycling in the rain was well and truly established.

I remember thinking whilst on the Budapest to Croatia trip that cycling across the USA was the biggie' and wondered if I could ever achieve it. I knew that unlike those tours that had taken place in the company of my favourite cycle friend, the USA would not be anything I could convince anyone to go on, becoming a solo trip. This led to the thought, 'did I even want to do a solo trip?', Would I cope with the expected loneliness? And most importantly 'would it be fun?'. The one thing I did know for sure was that it would take far longer than the max 3.5 weeks undertaken so far. It would be multiple months with time out of work, which was not financially viable at the time, easily burying the plan for the future.

Having not been able to extinguish this thought completely, I decided to answer this question to put it out of my mind for good. If I did go I would want to visit the places I hadn't been before, resulting in a northern route. Starting somewhere near Seattle, and visiting Montana and Yellowstone National Park, then continuing through the Midwest to Chicago, and finishing around Washington DC. It was either D.C or an extra 500 miles to Boston, making D.C the winner. I put the rough mileage into the calculator, divided by the 40 days I could manage workwise, resulting in an answer of 92 miles per day. CRAP! I remember saying out loud, that is indeed a mega challenge but not wholly impossible... I couldn't believe it, if it wasn't 'impossible' it was therefore doable and 'game on' from that moment. It was now just a question-of when and how.

THE WHEN?
AND HOW?

Although initially scary, having fixed parameters and less choice was the best thing to keep me on track with planning, pretty much dictating all the elements. In hindsight, having fixed parameters was definitely a blessing in disguise!

Here were the facts;

1. I had a mortgage to pay and students to get back to. This was not the time for an armchair travel moment putting pins in the map and saying 'lets go everywhere'. I had 45 days including flights, tops!

2. No time to faff around with flight connections or anything else, Seattle and Washington had direct flights and are places I always wanted to go. I desperately needed to see Montana, and Chicago seemed unavoidable on the map so that set the route. If there was something to see and prettier roads to ride I would divert, otherwise I would keep to a straight line as possible.

3. I needed to do big miles each day, approximately 80 to 90. I had done a couple of century day rides with the furthest of 88 on a cycle tour. This was the scariest and intimidating fact of all. Although plenty of people cycle these miles with a tourer type bike, for me this known and tested traditional pannier set up was too heavy and slow. I basically needed all the help I could get. I was taking my road bike and as little as possible!

4. This led to the inevitable conclusion that I was not going to be able to camp. Lightweight touring meant just that, no room for heavy gear, or seemingly anything. Can't say I was too disappointed, a shower and a proper bed seemed like a good plan and the 'safer' option, with the additional bonus of helping to appease my friends, and of course decreased the possibility of being eaten by a bear...

I figured a good starting point was to get excited and do some 'focussed' research. I devoured stories from well-known big record-breaking adventurers, to the inspiring 'triumph over adversary' tales and enthusiastic 'you-tuber' blogs. All of these journeys were very different, inspiring me on many different aspects of my trip. I -sought out as many books as I could on trail blazing female adventurers (of which I was pleased there are some to choose from), being in-awe and jealous of their abilities in equal measure! 'Why didn't I do this long ago?' I thought! However, there was one obvious difference from these women to myself. They were mostly athletes, ex-athletes and generally all round super fit people. Now, I'm a capable cyclist, but one look at me is all you need to rule me out of the 'super fit people' box. 'But

Hey, I've got to start somewhere' I thought', and being inspired was a good place to be. After much searching, I managed to find one book about a two-man 40 day road bike trip across the USA. This gave me hope and a bit of route information that maybe it wasn't too crazy a thing to do.

In amongst all these tales, the biggest influencing advice was to simply 'commit' to your plan, as that is the hardest bit. I mean I wasn't entirely sold that committing myself was harder than lugging myself over mountains, but I got the gist of the sentiment. I decided I would commit at least a year in advance, giving me enough time to plan and the best chance to train. It was early 2018, and looking forward I saw no weddings or any other unavoidable plans in the diary for the summer of 2019. It all seemed to fall into place and I had about 4 months before 'commitment time' was upon me. In truth, it was already a done deal, but some 'wiggle room' was comforting in case something unavoidable came up, or I decided to bottle it! The main hesitation was the obvious reality of how fit I needed to get in a short space of time. I've always been overweight, and at that particular time more so than usual. I have said many times before I would figure this out at some point. It was time to face up to this lifelong bad habit, and just get on with it. I was under no illusion that I would suddenly become an athlete, but this sudden dose of reality scaring me into action was just what the imaginary doctor ordered. The time had come, I needed an actual plan, and a good one at that!

THE THREE PART PLAN

One of my favourite books was Mark Beaumont's latest account of his new world record 'Around the World in 80 Days'. Although a huge sponsor supported trip with a massive team involved, it was impressive none the less and on the edge of human endurance and the height of logistical and practical planning. I would love to see that be broken one day, but you would either need to be rich or hold celebrity clout to get that sort of sponsorship to even think of undertaking it. Something which was impressed upon me from this account was that he achieved exactly what he set out to do. He made a plan and 'read it like a script', describing this as where the race was won, all in the planning. This played to my strengths, I love planning and set about writing my own 'script' that I could follow split into three distinct categories;

1. The Training
2. The Route
3. The Equipment

THE TRAINING

90 odd miles a day meant this trip needed to be as fast and therefore as 'lightweight' as possible. The heaviest thing going was myself by a long shot, and the hypocrisy in taking a carbon bike when the easiest way to be lighter is to lose the pounds. It was either laugh or cry with embarrassment, but I still needed to lose at least 1.5 stone before I went. The lighter I was, the easier and therefore more enjoyable the trip would be, not to mention less chance of injuries, it wasn't rocket science after all. I set myself the target of losing half a stone each term, which in normal people's time is about 3 or so months. This seemed a very reasonable target in terms of weight loss, and my reward would be to book the flights after 3 months in January 2019. If I couldn't achieve this by January, then I wasn't committed enough and wouldn't go, simple as.

The second thing was to exercise EVERYDAY. If I couldn't for whatever reason that was fine, I wouldn't rebuke myself for it, but every exercise session got logged in a chart, and any days off were obvious. I was already a regular cyclist but now I would cycle 'everywhere'. Over the preceding months the usual routes included massive diverts, with the 2.5 miles to the supermarket regularly turning into a 10 mile round trip. I begrudgingly chose to cycle home in the rain several times rather than get a lift. I lived in lycra, apologised for my appearance constantly, and got use to being constantly sweaty and smelly. I had cycled big miles on previous trips, therefore wasn't too concerned about the impending daily mileage. The bigger concern was doing it every day without getting injured. If I got injured either during training or on the trip it was likely to end in disappointment, and this was number one on my trip 'risk' list. Number two, three and four were 'getting run over by a truck', 'equipment failure' and non cycling health problems' such as sunburn, migraine and period issues. Something male cyclists definitely have an advantage on! To help with issue number one, I cross-trained adding gym sessions of swimming, running and anything but cycling to my routine.

This seemingly relentless routine continued for months with a few inevitable lapses in progress, mainly around Christmas, but I guess that was to be expected. I did commit to cycling every day of the Christmas holidays and have a lovely memory of lapping bushy park on Christmas day being entertained by thousands of 'park runners' dressed up as Father Christmas' with added buggy 'sleighs' and 'reindeer' dogs in tow! During those months, I could see my stats improve with an increased average speed, alongside more favourable numbers on the scales. This meant I could book the flights. My target in training was a consistent 15 miles per hour on all cycles, where I would push for more on shorter and flatter routes. This would inevitably go down when carrying kit, but consistency, not speed, was the key. Cycling around 12 – 13 mph on the trip would total approximately 7-9 hours of cycling each day plus breaks. On my previous tours I averaged about 55 miles a day, therefore needing to find another 35 miles a day. I figured I would do this by:

a) Being fitter
b) Weighing less
c) A lighter more efficient bike
d) Carrying as little as possible
e) The preferable road, weather and traffic conditions of the USA compared to Europe.

This seemed fairly logical to me, and I continued in this manner upping the mileage over time, adding in some long-distance cycling events here and there to keep me on track.

THE ROUTE

As mentioned, the excitement of planning a trip is not exactly a chore to me, and I spent many a happy late night staring at Google Maps. Calculating various elevation and mileage options, and moving the street view 'Google Man' into the map to check the road conditions and the potential view! A huge help in this planning was the USA website the 'Adventure Cycling Association'. With excellent information and detailed maps to view online, it quickly become my go to site. There are already many tried and tested long-distance routes, with the official 'Trans America' trail mapped out along the centre of the country, with alternate southern and northern options. I had already bought a road atlas of the USA and spent a couple of nights with a pink marker mapping various route options onto it. I then ripped out the pages and stuck the route onto my bedroom wall. To my surprise it took up the entire wall and was rather an intimidating sight to wake up to!

After much research, a rough route was decided on which pretty much adhered to the original plan. I did re-route my reasonably straight line East of Seattle to go north near the Canadian boarder to join the official 'northern route' for a week, before crossing diagonally through Montana and onto Chicago. From here, it seemed fairly straight forward to get to Pittsburgh, then follow the 'Great Allegheny Passage' all the way to Washington D.C. This long-distance cycle route utilising disused railway lines and a canal seemed the only plausible way for cyclists to get through the Appalachian Mountains which all roads seemed to avoid. Although a tow path, it would hopefully be a scenic, traffic free and happy way to end to the trip.

To add some flexibility into the trip, I decided to fully plan the first 9 days, and then follow my plan of where I 'should' make it to each day in order to keep me on track. As the first 9 days would take me over the Rocky Mountains in the height of tourist season, I decided to pre book accommodation as the thought of having no where to stay at the end of my day is not my idea of fun. I had briefly added up the rough cost of a motel each night, and at the going rates coupled with the worst exchange rate in history, thanks to Brexit, I was looking at nearly £2.5k just on accommodation. This was not an option and thankfully my saviour came in the form of the 'Warm Showers' website. This hosting platform works very similar to 'Couch Surfing', but exclusively for touring cyclists. How I did not know about this before was a mystery, and the ethos is right up my street. Not only would this solve some of my accommodation problems, it would also hopefully solve my need for people, and answer problem number two on my list 'being lonely'. In comparison, problem number one was being run over by a truck but wearing a bright jacket would have to do for this one. There were thousands upon thousands of people not just in America but worldwide on this app that put up cyclists for free, helping them out along the way, all for the 'paying it forward' ethos and love of humanity. This was instantly my new favourite thing, I signed up, and got emailing potential hosts.

I excitedly told everyone about this new find (which went down well), and I now had a rough plan the whole way across. I would generally avoid cities as they are slow, by keeping close enough to large towns in case I needed amenities. I planned stops roughly equidistant apart in towns where there was at least 1 motel. The only oddity was a couple of days through Wyoming and South Dakota, which were rather sparse in accommodation options. I resigned to figure out this problem when I was there, as constantly staring at the map was not producing any motels or solutions. I'm sure all would all be fine in the end, as after all this was a first world country, and either the kindness of strangers or credit cards would go a long way to solving these issues.

THE EQUIPMENT

The decision to take my road bike on a touring trip was proving very problematic when seeking information about gear. Advice (wanted or otherwise) from bike shops, forums and the general cycling community was that a road bike is not built for this type of trip and I should think again. To me, the theory was solid. The bike was fast, I loved riding it, it made me happy, and my aging hybrid bike was not up to the task. I was going with the emerging trend of 'bikepacking' bags over traditional pannier setup, and was excited to get some new gear.

This excitement was short lived when I found these bags are made for much larger bikes than my 48cm frame. The large 'abdomen' saddle bags needed more clearance between the saddle and the tyre than I had, and the front roll bags would not fit between my compact 'female' handlebars, alongside the frame bags needing a larger triangular space than my bike had. This took a lot of researching, measuring and thinking outside of the box to make something work. I emailed many companies to see what they had for a female geometry bike. They were very helpful in saying they could make me something bespoke or send things back free of charge if they didn't fit, but essentially it was a demand and supply issue.

After lots of time wasting, I ended up with an Alpkit 'Fiana' which made the clearance on paper, but in reality, was held up with a steel ruler inside and a piece of rope on the outside. This was a good quality waterproof bag though, and apart from it not fitting properly I was happy with it. I bought a cheap Chinese made triangle frame bag in small for £6.50, which was surprisingly good quality and looked like it would hold up well. My handlebar bag was an 'Ortleib accessories pack' that was meant to attach to the front of their specific roll bag. However, it was the only thing small enough of decent quality that would fit. The final piece was a Blackburn top tube bag. It didn't hold much but would be handy for snacks and small electrical items. I had toyed with the idea of wearing a Camelbak as in previous tours, but the extra weight on your back for big miles is not recommended, and it wasn't comfy. I was still madly testing things the week before I left, and was super proud of my set up, especially managing to fit two 500 ml water bottles in completely random places including under the frame. My new 'pimped up' bike looked a bit space-age and a world away from my previous trips. If the bike could talk, I'm not sure whether it would have been pleased or embarrassed by its new look!

My initial research into potential luggage options calculated a total capacity of approximately 25 -30 litres of space. The reality of what I ended up with was about 18 litres max by the time you roll up the ends properly so they are watertight. Clearly the items on my 'would like to take' list were sadly not going to make it. It was essential items only and some of those became debateable.

Whilst training, my mid-range bike gear bought on ebay and in the sales had never been a problem, and it always amazed me how much brands charged for such a small amount of lycra! £100 for some top level shorts, and well into the £100's for a fancy jacket! 'Are these really worth the money and had I been missing out?' I thought. One thing was for sure, as the miles increased so did the pain and discomfort in my undercarriage. At points I was googling to see if this was 'normal' behaviour and what the solutions were. Not wanting to go into too much detail here, but the problem seemed common in female cyclists with some even citing an operation to solve the pain. WHAT! I love my cycling but if that was the solution then I was happy to cycle less! Some fancy shorts and chamois cream would have to do. I bought two different pairs and the difference was clear from the outset. Better material, better fit, comfier on the bike, clearly I had been missing out. I followed this up with a fancy jacket that was light, waterproof, screw-up-able and in the most horrible 'coral' colour. A truck would be able to see me a mile away in this colour, and the chances of getting run over were getting slimmer! I added a bright helmet to the mix that clashed nicely with the jacket and my comical look was complete! I had turned into a proper branded lycra clad cyclist resembling the local cycle clubs I see going around in packs. Half of me felt like I had sold out, but I sure was comfy… and still didn't care to cycle around in packs, so clearly all was ok!

Although these new purchases reduced the bike pain, my saddle sores were getting worse. Now, if you don't know what these are your first thought is probably correct! Maybe a 'bike fit' might help to get everything in a good anatomically correct position, and a local one for £40 seemed worth a go. Although the guy was super helpful armed with fancy angle calculations on his ipad, the wider saddle suggestion and difference in saddle height was all too late. The small tweaks I was hoping for turned into decisions about the bike set up. Why had I done this so close to the trip, surely ignorance was bliss, right? In the end I decided changing a saddle, so close to going, was a very bad idea, and I modified the changes back to their original positions. Even if I wasn't riding in the 'correct' position, I had been doing it this way all my life and I figured I know my body and riding style better than anyone else, and also I had to put the saddle height back up in order to fit the saddle bag!

Another new problem that appeared in training was large amounts of pain in my feet. Seemingly this was called 'cyclist hot foot' created by swelling inside the shoe. Every shop assistant I sought advice from said I needed road shoes which would be less painful. However, as the cleats protrude out the bottom of these shoes walking 'normally' is not possible. With only one pair of shoes coming with me, I needed to go with mountain bike cleats that are indented into the shoe, thus allowing normal walking. Properly aligning these cleats and increasing shoe size should help. I ran out of time to test many and went with my least painful pair out of two. I figured I would be stopping more on the actual trip than in the training, hopefully relieving both the foot and the under carriage pain.

It was nearly time to go and I had sourced the majority of my stuff in the smallest and lightest versions I could find or afford. Now, I'm sure one women's list of essential items will differ greatly from another, and mine was looking bleak. How optional are toiletries and clothes? I could buy both out there so in this case very optional! I was sad that my electric toothbrush couldn't come, not even the handle of the manual toothbrush or comb made it. No need for unnecessary pointy things! I justified that two sets of bike clothes would be a good idea, plus they didn't weight anything. I added one non cycling shirt and pair of trousers, clearly I couldn't hang out on the plane or in people's houses in cycling gear, no need for such obscene behaviour! I would have to learn to love these now literal everyday clothes. No room for a hoodie of sorts, so the cycle jacket would have to double up as a normal jacket. Another notable exception was a little gas burner. The thought of having a nice cup of tea or basic 'boil in a mug' type food was a great pick me up for potential sad times and general self sufficiency. Absolutely no way I could justify this space and weight, unfortunately. I mean, only one pair of pants made the cut! If I needed another pair or anything else along the way, as mentioned, I'll just buy as I go along.

It was nearly time to go and I had sourced the majority of my stuff in the smallest and lightest versions I could find or afford. Now, I'm sure one women's list of essential items will differ greatly from another, and mine was looking bleak. How optional are toiletries and clothes? I could buy both out there so in this case very optional! I was sad that my electric toothbrush couldn't come, not even the handle of the manual toothbrush or comb made it. No need for unnecessary pointy things! I justified that two sets of bike clothes would be a good idea, plus they didn't weight anything. I added one non cycling shirt and pair of trousers, clearly I couldn't hang out on the plane or in people's houses in cycling gear, no need for such obscene behaviour! I would have to learn to love these now literal everyday clothes. No room for a hoodie of sorts, so the cycle jacket would have to double up as a normal jacket. Another notable exception was a little gas burner. The thought of having a nice cup of tea or basic 'boil in a mug' type food was a great pick me up for potential sad times and general self sufficiency. Absolutely no way I could justify this space and weight, unfortunately. I mean, only one pair of pants made the cut! If I needed another pair or anything else along the way, as mentioned, I'll just buy as I go along.

CLOTHING	BIKE	TOILETRIES	ELECTRONICS	MISC.
» Endura Bib Shorts	» Lock	» Deodorant	» Front Light	» Boris Bear (Mascot)
» Castelli Shorts	» Inner tubes x2	» Toothbrush	» Rear Light	» Passport
» Gore tops x2	» Puncture repair kit	» Mini Toothpaste	» Garmin Edge 25	» Spork
» Gore Jacket	» Quick Fix Patches	» Small shampoo	» Garmin cable	» Penknife
» Underwear x2	» Mini Tool	» Combe	» Headphone	» Duck Tape
» Cycle gloves	» Tyre levers x2	» Razor	» Phone	» Cable Ties
» Sunglasses	» Mini Pump	» Sun cream	» Power bank	» Pen
» Shoes	» Chain Lube	» Moisturiser	» Charging cable	» Mini first aid / medicine
» Helmet	» Pedal Spanner	» Chamois cream	» Plug adaptor	» Draw String Bag
» Buff				

For extra security, I duck-taped a zip lock bag into the inside of my handlebar bag to hide and secure my passport and cash. This handlebar bag was easily removable with a handy strap to sling over my shoulder. I had never owned a proper handbag before, I either travel about with my trusty rucksack or just a phone and keys. It seemed very fitting that this makeshift cycle one was my first handbag. I'd keep all my valuables in it and then popping into shops would be quick and easy.

So that was it, I was about ready to go! The only thing left was to dismantle the bike, carefully pack in into the cardboard bike box liberated from Halfords and pad out with my clothes. I was delighted it weighed 21kgs, with 2kgs to spare for my allowable limit. I had already declared to British Airways that my checked luggage was going to be a bike, which seems to be the only airline that take bikes without extra cost. In case I couldn't find anything to open the with the other end, I cut a flap in the box and duck taped the serrated spork inside, that would have to do! I wrote 'this way up' and 'fragile' over the box everywhere, just in case it made a difference. 'Right, that's it' I thought, there was nothing left to do and no point in wondering 'what if' about anything now. Let's get going on this adventure!

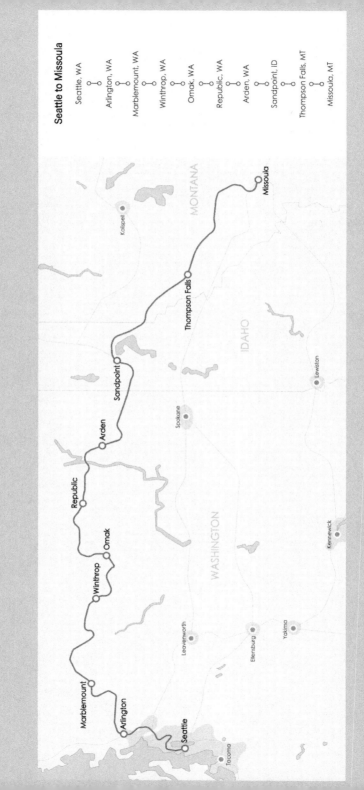

Seattle to Missoula

Seattle, WA
○─○
Arlington, WA
○─○
Marblemount, WA
○─○
Winthrop, WA
○─○
Omak, WA
○─○
Republic, WA
○─○
Arden, WA
○─○
Sandpoint, ID
○─○
Thompson Falls, MT
○─○
Missoula, MT

PART
2
OVER THE MOUNTAINS

DAY 0:
LYNE TO SEATTLE

boarded the uneventful flight wearing a comical mix of normal clothes and cycling gear, leading to many bizarre looks and questions. I didn't think there would be problem getting through Seattle airport, but had forgotten about the joy that is US customs! Due to a 'busy day' we all got held on the bridge between the plane and immigration for 40 minutes before embarking on the two hour switchback queue! Now, if I knew it was going to be 2 hours, I would have gone to the toilet first! Children were being lifted over people's heads and taken to the toilet by officials. I so wished I could get away with this, and I had to make do with jumping up and down instead, it was very nearly a very embarrassing start to the trip.

After the happy interaction with the customs official, I was reunited with my bike box that was lovingly waiting for me with not a mark on it. Trollies had been removed as there were too many people in the hall, adding to the unhappy chaos in the air. I dragged it to the member of staff that looked about 12, who was completely overwhelmed, and wearing an 'I'm here to help' badge. I felt like taking the badge from him and saying 'run for your life' but I politely said I would need to go through the disabled/exit lane in order to get through. 'No mam you need to join the line' he nervously told me. I insisted I wasn't trying to avoid the line and be a pain in the arse, it's just that my box will not fit through the switch backs. 'Is that not really obvious?' I thought. He called over help and 10 minutes of discussion ensued before another official finely stated the best solution was for me to go through the disabled/exit barrier. He seemed so pleased with this excellent 'brand new' solution. I smiled, and went through before anyone else could stop me. After dragging the box through multiple security doors and onto a train, I finally made the arrivals hall. Although awkward, I didn't mind dragging my box around, as it was a source of much amusement for others. Three different people all asked 'why did you bring such a big TV with you?' I informed them it was a bike and they seemed even more bemused replying 'why would you bring a bike?' 'Why would I bring a TV!' I replied. Bonkers! At least my accent was going down well.

If I hadn't read it in a blog you would have no idea there was a bike assembly at the terminal between carousels 9 & 10. It seemed the airports best kept secret and also the best thing ever! I quickly got to work putting the bike together (after fishing out the spork of course). Once finished, I had no idea what to do with the box, and slightly shamefully left it by the bike assembly area. My thoughts were that someone would appreciate it in disassembling their bike, or more likely the counter opposite that boxed up and stored people's items would make use of it. It could also be called littering, I'll let you decide...

The same blog that mentioned the assembly area, stated you could cycle out of the airport via a service road, which was already plugged into my Garmin. Unfortunately, upon my exit I was the wrong side of a large concrete wall with no way around, and all roads leading to the motorway. I told a lovely traffic lady about my plan who was super nice but informed me there was no way I was cycling out of here and would have to take the train. This was an excellent time to employ my favourite travelling 'rule of 3'. If you're unsure of the advice given, ask three people, then take that as the truth. Ten minutes later after having talked to two more officials, I made my way to the train! I consoled my 'inner self sufficiency voice' that I was already 2.5 hours behind schedule and I didn't 'need' to cycle to the city centre, and stop being so stubborn. I felt I would be having constant arguments with myself about such things all trip.

Literally lost on arrival in the middle of Seattle, I employed Google Maps to get me to the Space Needle my official starting point. I didn't have any data out here so following a not so accurate GPS dot took a long time. Now, just to be clear, anyone who was pedantic about cycling 'coast to coast' would say I needed to dip my tyres in both oceans each side or it just wouldn't count. Now, Seattle really isn't that kind of place with no obvious beach to do this from. It was clearly on the coast and that was good enough for me. I had previously dipped my tyre in the North Sea on a UK 'coast to coast' trip, which in reality meant clogging up your brakes with sand for the rest of the trip.

Not for me, a picturesque shot by the Space Needle would be far more pleasing than starting by some boggy industrial area.

After a starting photo at the surprisingly small Space Needle, I cycled the 2 miles to my amazing 'Warm Showers' hosts for the night. A lovely adventurous couple in a colonial style house boasting my own room and a wonderful view. I had totally fallen on my feet; they were so lovely and it was just what I needed to calm my nerves. I was here, everything was ok and the trip of a lifetime awaited tomorrow, or whatever time of day my body thought it was!

DAY 1:
SEATTLE TO ARLINGTON

A nd we're off! I had said my grateful goodbyes and started freewheeling down the road. Then... 'GEMMA!!' came a shout from behind me, and I saw my host waving my Garmin charging cable at me. Excellent I thought, nearly messed up the trip navigation on day one! My first aim was to get to a phone shop to purchase a USA sim-card. Was easy enough, put my mind at rest that I could call people on route if needed. This was more for emergency, I just wanted the sim for data! I had no room for paper maps and would be going through them so quickly it just seemed pointless. I would try and rely on Google Maps etc and pre-routing into my Garmin. I had chosen the Garmin 'Edge 25' due to its small and lightness. Its payoff is not having a map function but rather a small line to follow with arrows stating how many feet to the turning. This was always perfect for me, as the last thing I wanted to do was stare at tech rather than the surroundings. Coupling this with my usual good sense of direction, following signs, old-school asking people, and of course my nose, I'm sure I would be just fine.

I had routed some long-distance cycle paths out of the city and was very pleased to see that these were purpose built with cycle crossings and signs. Seattle is a well renowned 'cycle city' and I could see why, it wasn't the straightest route out but a pleasure calmly cycling through parks and avoiding the busy traffic. The mood of this lovely city cycle was only brought down by my saddle bag constantly hitting the back wheel when going over bumps. I stopped several times to tighten up the strapping but on one inspection found I had already worn a hole in the bottom of the bag. I was so annoyed with myself, but administered the duck tape and tightened the piece of rope. It was a good solution, but now the bag was not removable from the bike. My usual annoyance that everything is generally designed around the 'standard' (ie man) came back. 'Oh well' I thought, shorter people have less wind resistance, right? I'm not sure being tall has any benefits in the sport of cycling? Got to be one of the only ones that doesn't I thought, maybe that's why I do ok? We will wait and see…

I followed the 'Centennial Trail' out of the city, with flat perfect tarmac, water fountains and toilets. Toilets on a bike route? Decided to stop at each one knowing this was not the norm! When not on these lovely cycle paths, the roads were stress free with cars letting me go first at the lights and the seemingly illogical '4 way stops'. As I planned this as a 'take it easy' day, I couldn't have asked for a better one to get use to cycling on the 'wrong' side of the road'. I even had an extended lunch break in the lovely town of Snohomish, where I sat by the river watching skydivers land in the field opposite and read my book. I had planned on finishing it on the plane but that didn't happen, so it now took up way too much room in my allocated food bag. It seemed ludicrous that I didn't have any stuff but I had a heavy book. I would finish and off load asap!

My day finished at a 'Warm Showers' host in Arlington 59 miles from where I started. A great day and a good taster to Seattle life. With its modern culture, beautiful lakes and islands sandwiched between mountains, it was my kind of place and I could see why it's constantly ranked as one of the best cities to live in the USA.

DAY 2:
ARLINGTON TO MARBLEMOUNT

D ay two was all about prepping for day three, the big day, the scary one, and the one that I was 'bricking it' about since the start. The 90 miles wasn't the problem, the 7500 feet of elevation up and over the Washington pass certainly was. However, as any touring cyclist knows 'on paper' doesn't usually bear much relation to how hard or easy a day will be. The weather and road conditions are always a massive feature of the uncontrollable elements that make touring so exciting and unpredictable. I would prep as best as I could for the aspects I could control; then wing the rest of it, as normal. I had 56 miles to the 'Buffalo Inn' in Marblemount, the last accommodation option before the pass. This Inn, it's restaurant, and a couple of petrol stations were the only facilities until the other side. These didn't even open until 8am, therefore food foraging needed to happen today.

With only 56 miles I was looking forward to an easy day, spending time taking in the sights. Instead, I ended up spending this time in bed with a migraine. I tend to get migraines when my body is not happy and will generally be sick before starting to feel better. After several failed attempts to get going, I was finally sick and that was my cue to get on the bike. My host had left for work early, luckily leaving me with sick person privacy, and not having to deal with an ill tourist!

I don't remember much about the morning apart from feeling awful, but a lunch time stop in the town of Darrington, complete with local people chit chats made me feel much better about life. I loaded up with a US sized pasta salad and sandwich which both ranked high on the 'squashabilty' meter. The price of food (and everything else) was just so expensive, with 'Brexit' looming the pound had fallen to its lowest rate against the dollar since records began. I just had to accept this was going to be a very expensive trip and get over it. The afternoon was much more pleasant and I cheered myself up with my number one happiness inducer, singing along to my favourite tunes! The cycle paths of the cityscape soon changed into roads cutting through pine forests, winding around lake shores as the beautiful mountains grew nearer. The beauty of mountains, forests and lakes never gets boring to me and I could stare at them all day. I rolled into Marblemount about 5pm although it took me another hour to actually make it into my room. The Inn's reception was located at the restaurant about 100 meters down the road from the sleeping part. Not that convenient when you can't find your room… In the end the magic way in was up the stairs behind a door with a completely different number, so obvious when you know?! Dinner that night was the biggest meal I had ever seen, which easily defeated me.

DAY 3:
MARBLEMOUNT TO WINTHROP

Either jet-lag or nervousness meant I was already awake at the 04.30 alarm. After way far too much faffing I made it out the door into the rain at 05.15 complete with my draw string bag of food and extra water. I passed the 'North Cascades Visitor Centre' after 15 miles, and stopped for 2nd breakfast at Diablo lake. The view across the lake as I started to climb was just beautiful, and with no other vehicles on the road the peacefulness was something to take in. There were a few mountain tunnels with cyclists' buttons that warn vehicles of a cyclist presence as it was pitch black inside. My front light had already ran out of charge but there were going to be no vehicles coming this way over the pass for hours. I pressed every one of these tunnel's buttons anyway just for fun.

The 'top' of today's climb was at roughly mile 57 and I wondered whether knowing this, added to the adventure or not. One thing was for sure, it's so hard not to look these things up and definitely makes the planning easier, but some of the spontaneity has gone. I'm sure this balance between planning and spontaneity would sort itself out along the trip, but for now having mile 57 in my sights was a good thing. The gradient of the climb is described as 'railroad' at approximately a steady 6% incline. Sometimes it was hard to tell that the road was going up at all other than I was churning out between 5 and 8 mph. Hardly going anywhere per hour is a bit demoralising and taking nearly 4 hours to go those last 27 miles was a proper slog. I remember seeing the turn off to the viewpoint when nearly at the top and thinking they were unnecessary miles and I didn't need to do it. I was so chuffed I did - the view was just stunning. Celebratory biscuits were a must whilst I sat there looking at the impending downward road on the other side.

My joy of the downhill lasted about a minute until I turned the corner and was hit with a massive crosswind. Combining this with stones all over the road, it took all my concentration to keep the bike in a straight line. My hands hurt from constantly pulling the breaks with my eyes were watering from the wind and constant stone watching, this was not a time for blinking! I only managed 40 mph before I was 10/10 on the 'poop my pantsometer'. 40mph is a very rare thing in the UK for me, with bad road conditions and general lack of straight lines. I can only ever remember doing it once in Devon, where a cattle grid suddenly appeared causing much panic and nearly coming unstuck. My friend did much the same but also being stung by a bee at the same time! After the windy steep part was done and my confidence returned, the run into Winthrop was just amazing. I couldn't believe the speed that I was going, averaging over 20 mph for the last 30 miles. I had the best tail wind and was simply loving life. I knew I would likely regret being sunburnt later, but I couldn't stop - I was on a roll.

The town of Winthrop looked just like something out of the Wild West, with saloon style buildings, a variety of vehicles parked everywhere and happy people eating ice-creams in the sunshine. The illusion of this Wild West façade was later burst by finding out it was purpose built to bring in the tourists. Well, it worked with me and everyone else I guess. My hosts were a lovely retired couple who were very surprised I had made it by 15:30, 'them and me both' I thought! I was informed I had lucked out with my tailwind as its usually a headwind, and I had clearly lucked out on being allowed to stay here. Their house was a self built 'off grid' beauty boasting its own power supply, water well and vegetable garden. That evening I was fed an amazing home-grown meal with excellent conversation and picked up loads of lovely messages from home. I made a little video saying if I could make it through this day then I could make it through the whole thing. I couldn't be happier and went to bed on a high.

DAY 4:
WINTHROP TO OMAK

My high carried on into the morning whilst enjoying a lovely breakfast finding out about life in this area. They were retired physicians having spent their careers working all over the country, moving here some years back. David would spend his time creating amazing things in his workshop, from the table and chairs we were sitting on, to the kitchen, and most of the house itself. They seemed to have a really great setup living the 'good life', something that massively appealed to me and made a great impression on my thoughts as I cycled away.

I headed through the valley towards Twisp then over the 'Loup Loup' pass. The scenery was just breath taking with birds of prey, rolling fields and picture perfect farms. I passed the 'smokejumpers' base where firemen are trained to parachute into the non accessible 'burning' areas to tend to wildfires. What a job that would be, I would certainly volunteer for that if I ever made it through their long waiting list to join! In fact, I would not have been able to do this route the previous year due to the widespread forest fires of 2018. Again, I felt luck was on my side and I would ride with it until it ran out!

I had left at 08.30 this morning which wasn't 'late' but meant I would be climbing the pass in the heat of the day and today was going to be a scorching 35 degrees. I was soon sweating all over the road with sun cream dripping everywhere, then managing to run out of water. I diverted to a campsite where a resident literally ranted at me for being a crazy Brit cycling in this heat and that I would rather starve than drink the water here. I didn't think it was worth arguing that on any given day I would likely drink or eat anything, and gratefully accepted a bottle of ice cold water from her cooler!

Once over the pass I had another go at getting to grips with controlling the bike at speed. I strapped my phone onto the front of my bag to see if I could get some downhill footage. It sort of worked with me holding it a little before pulling an emergency stop on the site of a large black object heading its way onto the road. 'A BEAR, AN ACTUAL BEAR'. I was so hoping to see one and it didn't disappoint. What a moment to have my phone strapped onto the front of the bike, it really was my lucky day! It looked like it might have been a baby bear, and likely not to appreciate having a camera in its face. I thought it was best not to 'poke the bear' so to speak, and who knew where mummy and daddy bear were lurking. I gave it a wave as I cautiously cycled by, not sure why, maybe I thought it would wave back? This kept me going for the rest of the baking hot but short day's ride. I got to the motel in Omak at 13.30 after 50 miles thinking that I overestimated the need for a shorter recovery day. I guess you only know you're over doing it when you get sick or gain an injury, and that probably was not a good barrier to push in week one. I'll chill anyway and recover from the bear overexcitement instead. Mandatory relaxing is not something I'm good at, but did my best with watching awful movies, eating and hours of planning the days ahead.

DAY 5:
OMAK TO REPUBLIC

was raring to go in the morning and surprised I was not first in the queue for the 06:00 'free' breakfast. Can't say it was exciting, but it was food. I discovered what the staple American breakfast item of 'gravy and biscuits' actually was. It was neither the sort of biscuits or gravy that we love in the UK, more of a sloppy porridge poured onto beige rusks, I gave that a miss. The waffle making machine looked like a messy health hazard to a newbie. So I gave that a miss too and went for the universal toast and coffee. 'Drip Coffee' as they call it was on tap with endless refills and something I was clearly going to get addicted too. I could feel the start of a new bad habit coming on.

It was 24 miles to Tonasket with rolling hills, and if you ignored the busy highway quite lovely indeed. I couldn't believe how hot it was, even for early in the morning, finishing all my water on arrival. After a rest and liquid top up, I had the pass to tackle with 28 miles of climbing, then the final 13 to Republic. I put my headphones on and sung along to some cheesy tunes on the way up. There was no way I was going to see any bears today unless they were interested in a fabulous Cher impression. To further distract me I did my first 'on the bike vlog' (which at this time I still called a blog), and told my friends of my frustration of going downhill only to have to make that elevation back up. If I wasn't struggling with the heat, I might have enjoyed the challenge more.

My other conversation point was to proclaim my new trip slogan I'd been coming up with. The happier I am the less I concentrate on the miles and everything else would just fall into place. After all, 'being happy' was my second trip priority after 'personal safety', I had to put these priorities first, not only because it's obvious, but I knew the 'race' element would become a personal obsession otherwise, potentially leading to silly decisions. My slogan was to stop whenever I wanted, speak to as many people as possible, smile always, and sing my way up the hills. In short, 'stop, speak, smile and sing'. This was to become a great comforter and positive mental strategy in the weeks ahead.

I reached the town of Republic by mid-afternoon and chilled in a coffee shop for a while. My hosts for that evening were an 'All American' couple just outside of town, obviously up a large hill. What I mean by 'All American' is; Flags flying, RV owning, Harley Davidson riding, hunting, shooting, fishing, loud, proud and unapologetic. What a fabulous place to be, and a complete contrast to my stay a couple of nights ago. I was quickly learning that this was the wonderful part about staying with warm showers hosts. Everyone is so different and whether their philosophies align or not with my own, the open and welcoming nature of this community was a fab way to learn about different cultural norms and was smashing my perceptions. What a surprise hit this community was becoming on my trip, and it was only day 5.

Boyd was a retired 'miner' who had worked all over the world. We talked late into the night over a wonderful dinner about everything and anything. He challenged my lifestyle, and I challenged him right back with an inquisitive nature and friendly banter. I learnt so much about the US political system and how everything seems to come down to politics, both State and Federal. Of course, politics runs everything back home to, but when you can drive across the entire country in less than a day, the differences seems small in comparison. Imagine trying to run and unite a country the size of Europe and getting policies to be accepted by all people? The drama of Brexit tells you how that might go. I now knew how the 'Electoral College' worked, what the Senate did, and something about the 'House of Representatives'. It was so utterly different to the UK system, I wondered how our two countries could be seen as 'similar' by the rest of the world. The US political system seemed so unfair and unjust depending on where you lived, and overall completely bonkers! I thought about all the unanswerable questions for hours in the coming days, I'd have to quiz some more people along the way.

I went to bed far later than I needed that night, but without a ride on the Harley. I did my best but something about a licencing law meant I couldn't. I'll save that one for another time.

DAY 6:
REPUBLIC TO ARDEN

There was no way that my gracious host was letting me get away early today. I was presented with the yummy local speciality of huckleberry pancakes for breakfast. Whilst deciding how much to eat was too much, I got a crash course in the mining industry, the local history of the logging industry and of course gun law! I could see the time ticking away on the clock behind him, and after an hour I felt rude to end the chat, but I just had to get going. I ran around looking for my cycle gear that had disappeared from its strategic drying position. I eventually found them in the garden making friends with the chickens. After brushing off the chicken feathers and deposits, I grabbed my bike to find a chicken sleeping on my saddle surround in poop! I was starting to love the randomness of this trip!

After about 7 miles I reached the road works that, I had been warned, would hamper me for much of my day. Once through and the traffic had long since passed, I realised there was no traffic coming the other way. They were clearly waiting for me before letting the oncoming traffic through. There was no sign of the end and it just had to be up hill. I felt awful holding everyone up and pumped my legs as quick as I could speeding up from about 5 mph to a whooping 8 mph! In what seemed a very long time later, I saw the guy the other end, and not wanting to lose face I kept my tortoise like sprint going until I heard him say into his radio "yep she's finally made it". 'Finally made it' I thought, laughing through the sweat dripping off me, cheeky whatsit! The queue was extremely long and I tried to avoid eye contact with any of the frustrated drivers as I did a little 'sorry' (not sorry) thank you wave!

After another couple of miles I came to the next queue cycling straight to the front. The man holding the Stop/Go sign was visually striking - looking like a cross between Santa and a garden gnome. He was just so bizarre looking and stood perfectly still starring straight over my head, I wondered for a moment if he was real and not a large garden gnome. 'Morning' I said mainly to dispel the silence, to which he replied 'morning mam' without a flicker of movement or eye contact. This awkward silence pursued for a few minutes before a pickup truck came down the hill behind him. Santa suddenly sprung into life with "mam we're gonna have to haul your bike up the hill". I thanked him for the offer stating I would be fine cycling and the cars behind could just go by. "Mam that's a really neat looking bike and we have wet tar all over the road, if you get any on your tyres you're really going to screw that thing up". An excellent point well made. I could see protesting wasn't going to work, and reluctantly took up the offer knowing he was just being polite and it was the truck or nothing. A soon as I dismounted, my bike was put in the pickup quicker than I could say 'please be careful', and off we went.

After a couple of miles weaving through the machinery I was placed back on the road. That lasted all of about 5 minutes before the next queue and pickup truck awaited. This time a lady approached (who also had slight gnome like attire) and said very politely "mam I would really like to take your bike up the road today", "is that a question?" I thought. I did my best British polite and smiley protesting tactic, but this time it was likely I might get squished by the machinery. What she really wanted to say was "you're really slow, completely in the way and holding everyone up, so get in the damn truck!". You've got to admire the customer service of the Americans! That lift was another 4 or so miles, leaving an hour's climb to the top. I felt really bad about getting the lift but I had no choice, and secretly quite enjoyed the whole episode. On the descent, the devastation from the previous year's forest fires was quite a sight and totally humbling.

The last 20 miles of the day was accompanied by a strong headwind and scorching heat. It took about 2 hours to do those last 20 and hard going. My hosts joined in with all the previous ones by living at the top of a hill. I had to stop 3 times in the last two miles just to rest and get my breath back. The heat was destroying me quickly and it was hard to be chirpy and grateful on arrival. Another wonderful house that they had purpose built, boasting a beautiful wrap around veranda looking out onto an orchard with mountains in the backdrop. What a beautiful spot and a kind couple I had to spend my evening with. On arrival I had spied a ukulele, guitar and assorted music books hanging around the living room, and wondered if I should mention what I did for a job. Thinking that this would likely come up in conversation anyway I got the ball rolling. Paula was part of a ukulele club and we spent the evening on the veranda playing tunes, singing and laughing... just perfect! I made a mental note to always cycle the extra miles (no matter how hilly it was) to stay with people, rather than selling out on a convenient motel. These are the experiences that make cycle touring just the best, the actual cycling is only the half of it.

DAY 7:
ARDEN TO SANDPOINT

Managed to leave at an acceptable 7.30 this morning with my hosts trying to poke cereal bars and fruit into every spare pocket of my jersey and bags, so sweet! I was trying not to take it all in the likelihood it would end up as a squishy mush, but I'm so glad I did as by the top of the first climb at mile 45 I had eaten it all! It was beautiful but a hard, hot slog of a climb. During the downhill I was in quite a lot of pain in my feet. The cyclist 'hot foot' problem was back and had to stop several times to get out of the heat. Whilst stopping I picked up some bad news about a friend's health at home, and sat under a tree for quite a while feeling very insignificant and very much in the wrong part of the world. Kicking around the pinecones, shouting and being miserable about this really wasn't productive, so I cracked on until the supermarket in town where I had a proper timeout from the heat and cycling. I bought the biggest bucket sized cold drink available and spent time texting friends which was exactly what I needed. My extended stopping and chatting took me straight into the heat of the day for the last 30 miles into Sandpoint, but today

I needed this time out. I would just have to employ the sing and smile part of my motto for the afternoon.

I knew I was coming out of the main mountainous part of the trip today and this was obvious when I joined my first highway. Something I would have to get use to from hereon in. This did speed up proceedings and in less than 2 hours I had reached my hosts at 5.30pm, and I could finally stop. I had cheered up by this time as I completely forgot I was entering the state of 'Idaho' today claiming my first 'state sign' picture. It felt exciting to be in a new state and a great sign of positive progress. My hosts were, again, lovely and greeted me with the same question that all the other hosts had. "Where is your stuff? Is that it?". These keen cyclists were used to people turning up with the traditional pannier set up and usually in pairs. I was the first 'lightweight tourer' on a road bike they all had hosted, and I'm sure the first solo female too. Much of the lovely conversation over dinner centred on these two topics, and I hoped in years or decades to come that 'female cyclists' could be known simply as 'cyclists'. I was happy in the hope that I was moving this along in my quest.

After dinner, we walked to a local bar where some classical music students were performing an impromptu gig. The bar was housed in an old barn next to a disused railway line that now doubled as a cycle track. A chilled evening ensued including the randomness of a French horn and bassoon duet cementing my fondness for this town. It wasn't that late when we returned, and was glad my hosts were keen to go to bed, as was I after the heat, hills and 91 miles.

DAY 8:
SANDPOINT TO THOMPSON FALLS

Trains, trains, trains! This is the lasting memory of my one and only day in Idaho as I crossed its northern 'pan handle'. I spent the morning skirting around the beautiful lake 'Pend Oreille' on Highway 200 which crossed back and forth over the railway line. The freight trains were straight out of the Wild West and seemed to go on forever. I spent much time happily wasting my energy on attempted train racing in order to get a wave or the jack pot of a 'toot toot' on the horn! I could have done this all day long and the stunning scenery did a good job of distracting me from the discomfort of overheating. I could have followed Highway 200 all the way to Thompson Falls, however, there was an inviting 'local' road the other side of the river that looked quieter. This road was a blissful 20 miles where more train racing ensued before suddenly…. the road ran out. A loose gravel track continued and I kicked myself for going rogue and coming off the highway. After less than a minute on this track, my front bag was in a continual state of coming loose and I had already veered into a bush twice, trying to catch it. I checked Google and although I had no signal, the blue GPS dot on a very grainy map could always be counted on for vague location awareness. Although I couldn't tell how far exactly, there was a junction ahead. I then noticed my blue dot sitting on the boarder line between Idaho and Montana. I guess the road running out was the border, 'What a lovely welcome to Montana this was' I thought, as I cracked on up the road lamenting being on the wrong side of the valley and missing the state sign. After what seemed liked ages, (but likely only a couple of miles), I made the junction and whooped at the sight of a proper road. My arms were aching, I had changed to a dusty shade of brown, and one of my water bottle cages was now in the drawstring bag having snapped off along the way! I thought it best not to chance this side of the valley again and backtracked to the nearest bridge crossing back onto Highway 200.

The next 50 miles would have been more glorious riding if it wasn't for the absolute oven I was riding in! Added to this was the annoyance of my dusty bike squeaking and protesting the whole way. The heat was tough, however, it was still just beautiful and had to be my most scenic (and hottest) day of the trip so far. It felt a shame to end the day at a motel with the only food option coming from the local gas station, but I was happy and importantly out of the sun! I spent the evening stripping and cleaning the bike and doing a marvellous fix 'if I do say so myself' securing the bottle cage back on with cable ties and duck tape. So glad I had brought these two magical fixing items! Today it had taken me 11 hours to do the 90 miles, which wasn't great, but a good reminder that times are irrelevant, I just had to make it from A to B each day. Logical of course, but looking at stats was a habit I was finding very hard to get out of.

DAY 9:
THOMPSON FALLS TO MISSOULA

The first job of the day was to cycle to the next town in time for breakfast. Nothing better than hunger to get me out of bed at 5.30am, clip on the lights and cycle off into the dark. It's such a beautiful 'still' time of day with no traffic to disturb the daybreak and sunrise ahead, a lovely benefit that never occurred to me when choosing to cycling eastwards. The 25 miles flew by, and once refuelled I mounted the bike for the next stint just as the sun disappeared behind clouds. 'Yes Clouds!', I hadn't seen any in days and took them as some sort of sign racing off before they disappeared. I hammered on as fast as I could feeling great, and cycling the whole 42 miles to the 'Windmill Bakery' in super quick time without stopping.

I had heard that this bakery in the middle of nowhere was worth a stop, and on arrival there was already a queue coming out of the door. Where had all these people come from? It's clearly the place to be and worth the travel. I joined the queue and got chatting to everyone attempting to answer their many questions. Luckily, there was a map on the wall forming a nice visual aid for my explanation. I asked what there was to buy as all I could see was lady madly preparing food behind a table, with a gentleman working a very simple till. "Oh, you just get whatever comes out of the oven or fryer" people told me. Ok random, but lack of choice is always an easy choice, and before I got to the till the lovely guy in front bought me an enormous warm donut, along with a cookie and coffee. Amazing! I'm not a donut fan at all, but this one was converting me, there was nothing not to like about this fried sugary – and free - delight! Had to be my best random lunch stop so far.

The afternoon's stint into the state capital of Missoula was a different setting. The clouds had gone, the temperature was back to 32 degrees, and the quiet pretty roads quickly turning into a highway going from 1 lane to 4 each way over the next 40 miles. This onslaught to my senses was becoming way too much and I counted down the miles for the rest of the day.

My host for the evening who also lived up the biggest hill in Missoula, was a lovely guy who used to be the boss of the Adventure Cycling Association, the company I had used for much trip research. I sought him out after a tip off from my hosts in Seattle and was glad he was available. We spent the evening having a look at my route and gaining many useful insights for the days ahead. I also found out that I was oblivious to the time zone I had travelled through the day before. Therefore, my getting in late time was not actually as bad as I had thought, bonus!

DAY 9.5:
REST DAY

As I had made Missoula as planned, I was rewarded a scheduled rest day, and this city was an excellent place to spend it. I took the free bus into the town, which sported cycle lanes everywhere and hardly any traffic to speak of. My first stop was a visit to the headquarters of the 'Adventure Cycling Association' for a nose around. Unfortunately, there was no information on my planned route across middle America, as they were currently researching the 'best route' which would be published in a couple of years. They were a friendly bunch though, and I got my picture on the wall of people cycling across the country, and a free ice-cream, you can't argue with that! I spent the rest of the day in various coffee shops planning my route and stays for the next week, and embarrassingly falling asleep! I loved everything about this city in my very brief visit, especially remembering the urban deer that roam the streets and gardens. It seemed there was no impatience for them at all, they are protected and a reminder that nature rules in this part of the world.

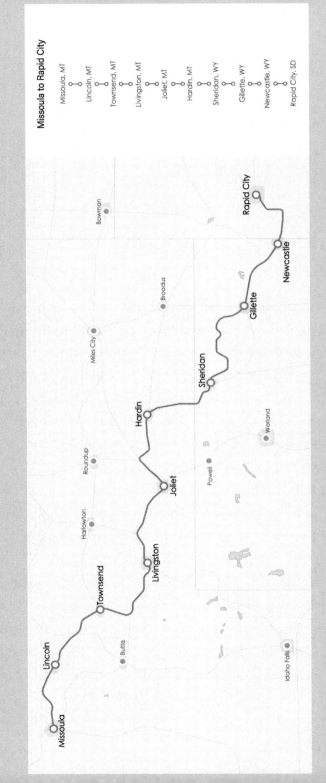

Missoula to Rapid City

- Missoula, MT
- Lincoln, MT
- Townsend, MT
- Livingston, MT
- Joliet, MT
- Hardin, MT
- Sheridan, WY
- Gillette, WY
- Newcastle, WY
- Rapid City, SD

PART
3
COWBOY COUNTRY

DAY 10:
MISSOULA TO LINCOLN

needed to gather some supplies before leaving including essential sun cream, so leaving super early was thwarted slightly by waiting for Walmart to open. The wait was worth it for the amazing purchase of factor 100 sun cream! What a find, who knew this existed, it could have doubled up as white paint, and had its own unique look especially after melting onto my lycra. The day's 85 miles were mainly uphill as I crossed the 'continental divide' or 'great divide' that serves as the Rockies highest point. With beautiful vistas interspersed with the occasional 'town', also known as a 'teeny tiny hamlet', mostly just a bar or a gas station. I sadly had no need of my new favourite habit of 'second lunch' after ordering the world's largest omelette at first lunch. Along with the beautiful scenery, I entertained myself by listening to audio books and remembering things to say for my evening 'vlog'. This little Whatsapp group of my friends was turning out to be fantastic motivation and entertainment for me, whilst hopefully being entertaining and occasionally informative back home. I never planned to be a 'vlogger' as it's the sort of word I hate, but after sending a video of my first day it's become a fantastic nightly habit. Anything funny got included in the vlog, with today's showcasing the wonderful decoration of the 'Three Bears Inn'. Everything was 'Bear' and 'Moose' themed from the bed spread to the toilet roll holder. Totally worth the extra $5 this motel cost compared to its nearest rival. The day's feelings were summarised in the nightly vlog stating 'I'm falling in love with Montana, it's just so beautiful....until it gets too hot to care about anything else!'.

DAY 11:
LINCOLN TO TOWNSEND

Another early start today leaving in shivering cold darkness. This had to be better than being fried alive, but it didn't seem like it at the time. The beautiful morning unfolded with 50 miles of jaw dropping scenery and hardly a car in sight. I reached the top of 'Flesher Pass' my highest point over the 'Continental Divide' at 6131 feet. The welcome downhill was a fantastic ride with perfect tarmac and speeds topping 40 mph plenty of times. The roads out here really do show up the pot-holed messes back home.

I was heading towards the city of Helena, where the beautiful roads turned 'city' very quickly, snapping me back into reality with oversized trucks and roads filled with rubbish. Coupling this with the returning heat and the general horribleness of the area, it was everything I hated about cycling. It was only 11.15 when I stopped and therefore lunch was still breakfast time with pancakes and eggs. I had had enough already and aborted my plan to see the centre of Helena, heading out on the quickest route towards my end destination of Townsend. I had mentally stopped and those 40 miles were hard going - flagging several times. I talked myself up off the roadside whilst consuming all my 'emergency' energy bars to keep me going. I'm sure the change of scenery was much to do with my mental flag as general tiredness was. There was one nice moment during this time, whilst waiting at the lights, a small child took pity on me and passed a donut through the window. I just about managed to grab it shouting 'thank you' before the car sped away. How lovely! That kind act managed to put the smallest of smiles on my face to get me through the afternoon.

DAY 12:
TOWNSEND TO LIVINGSTONE

I woke early tippy-toeing round my host's house in the dark, trying (and failing) not to bang into everything. My main concern wasn't waking my hosts, but their massive, overactive and rather intimidating dog! We'd met the night before, playing a trying game of 'get off my bed', followed by 'stop chewing my stuff' which the dog enjoyed muchly. I generally love dogs, but meeting this one in the 5.30am darkness was not on my to do list, and slipped out as quietly as I could.

The first 30 miles or so were mainly uphill and for whatever reason I was not happy on the bike. My feet and undercarriage were painful, and the road just keep going up. After many false 'tops' and using up all my distraction tricks, I stopped and sat at the side of the road quite depressed. The next 70 miles seemed an impossible task, I was completely done and contemplated how I could hitch a lift and re-route the next couple of days. After a while of overly dramatic 'the world is ending' thoughts, I gave myself a proper talking to. "You're in a gorgeous place, you've chosen to be here, it's not even that hot and you're sitting on your arse at the side of the road having a whinge". Time to woman-up and crack on. I needed to be in a happy place and reluctantly got up and started screaming as loud as I could in the middle of the road. "Why not? There's no one here?". The ridiculousness of the jumping and screaming at no one situation, soon turned into fits of giggles. I quickly put on some of my favourite tunes and picked up the bike. I was going to sing and dance my way to the next town 37 miles away, it almost sounded like fun…

I really did pull out all the stops for this effort, and sung as if no one could hear, standing up on the pedals, throwing shapes, and air guitaring as much as I could. On the odd occasion a car passed me I just added more gusto to the routine! The looks I got were just the best, I must have looked like the biggest wally in the state! A title I was happy to have, and finally reached the café for a very very extended stop. It didn't matter than the only items on the menu were 'fried things with cheese', my coffee cup was getting constantly refilled just like the movies, luckily no one wanted to talk to me, and I happily ate my fried cheese in peace.

I was heading for a Warm Showers host 15 miles outside of the town of Livingston. These miles were a detour that would need to be retraced in the morning and I was counting on this being a good call. I tried to ignore the disregarded motels in Livingston as I cycled out of town into a rainy headwind. This detour headed for the north entrance to 'Yellowstone National Park', a place I was desperate to go to. I had tried so hard to figure out how to make this happen but alas there were 3 main problems I couldn't figure out. Firstly, the official park lodges were booked up and I didn't have any camping gear. Relying on the kindness of strangers to invite me into their RVs for the night, or sleep rough, seemed a step too far. Secondly, it was at least 135 miles from the north gate to the west gate, with seven thousand feet of elevation in between. It would be a mammoth day that only scratched the surface of the park, missing the main must see areas. Thirdly, being the height of summer, large vehicles and winding roads make it a very dangerous place for cyclists to be. Finally, the extra routing to get in and out would add multiple days to the trip that I couldn't spare. I wanted to do this beautiful part of the world justice and it would just have to wait for another time, and I needed to let it go. Easier said than done cycling passed the 'Yellowstone' signs that pointed to the mountains ahead. I made a pact with myself that one day I'll come back and follow those signs.

Further up the road, I spied a man ahead waiting by the side of his truck looking straight at me, and as I got closer he greeted me warmly with 'Hello Gemma!' Initially a bit surprised to be recognised, but I wasn't exactly incognito and the chance of mistaking me with another female cycle tourer out here was exactly zero. It was My host Dane and he gave me directions to his house while he went into town for some supplies. I was to make myself at home and he and his wife would be back soon. What a top guy, I instantly cheered up and was completely stunned on pulling into their drive. In front of me was the house of my dreams, a small ranch style property complete with a wrap around balcony looking out to the beautiful valley surrounded by stunning mountains on either side. If I was to pick a spot and design a house it would not be as good as this, there was no question that travelling here was worth the extra miles. A perfect evening of wonderful conversation ensued in this lovely setting. I learnt so much about the local area, the people who live here, one of which just happens to include the fabulous guitarist John Mayer, and all about the wider Yellowstone area. They agreed with me that it was not a good idea to cycle through the park, as I would likely get run over by the inexperienced tourists driving oversized RV's. It was nice to get some reassurance on this, and I very much enjoyed my night in paradise.

DAY 13:
LIVINGSTONE TO JOLIET

O n paper this day was a long one, over 110 miles skirting the Interstate 90. My lovely host offered to give me a lift back to yesterday's turn off. "No!", I exclaimed as that would be cheating, but as it was backtracking it's not technically 'cheating' I thought. I could definitely do with the help today and placed the bike in the pickup. I did not want to leave this place at all, looked back the whole time and instantly missed my new friends once the turnoff appeared. What an emotional rollercoaster these adventures are, but I've always said it's better to leave a place before you want to, than outstay your welcome. I just wanted a few hours more.

Today's new challenge, to focus me, was knowing I had to go on the Interstate 3 times in the day, as the frontage road (the old highway) ran out several times. Cyclists are not allowed on USA Interstates apart from this bit in Montana, as basically they have no choice and will have to anyway, which is exactly was I was going to do, but nice to know I wouldn't be breaking the law doing it. I donned the bright jacket and glasses mirror that I was given back in Washington State for these sections. My concerns came from the build-up of other peoples' opinions of what is 'safe' rather than the reality. I did not feel unsafe at all, and I would easily take this than cycle though a UK city in rush hour. Although the thundering massive trucks seemed a scary idea, they were not that close and on the other side of the rumble strip. The actual concern was all the rubbish and debris in the hard shoulder, creating a rather annoying and technical slalom course. Most obstacles were the huge discarded tyre treads, making me question how so many trucks could have blown their tyres on this road? I later found out that these trucks have layers of tires that shed like snake skin whilst on the move. No wonder no one has cleared these up, they were a puncture waiting to happen, and after a stop I did indeed return to a flat tyre. It was the front tyre so much easier to fix and I was back on the road in 10 minutes.

Overall, the main day's riding was not that exciting, passing through many a small rundown railway town, that were now surplus to requirements with the coming of the interstate. Most of my entertainment was spent watching the trains which somehow never seemed to get boring, and re reading many messages whilst on the bike. Everyone's positivity never failed to cheer me up, I was so far away but felt so loved, what an excellent use of technology!

Upon reaching the large town of Columbus I was so tired and hot I could only think of one thing. Another amazing piece of technology…. Air conditioning! I took refuge in a supermarket with a bucket sized ice cold drink. I had another 20 hilly miles to my next hosts in the town of Joliet, and couldn't say I was looking forward to the prospect. Little did I know that waiting for me up the hills was a swarm of grasshoppers, literally thousands upon thousand in biblical proportions. There was not a lot to do about this but keep going. They covered the road, were all over me, and trying not to run them over was almost impossible. I've never cycled through a swarm of insects before, it certainly kept me on my toes flicking them off, and generally flailing about. I was glad to see the back of them once they swarmed off, not an experience to be recommended.

The small town of Joliet is out of the way from the main state routes, and had a lovely local feel. I was my hosts' first cycle tourist and they went out of their way to make me feel comfortable and at home. This carried on into the evening where their friends joined us for dinner and cards. One was a cyclist and brought his road pump along to get my tyres back up to pressure. No matter how much gusto I put into it, my arm just couldn't get the tyres above 80 psi with my mini pump. We chatted about bikes for a while as I embarrassingly tried to clean off the remains of many a grasshopper! Another of their friends organises a multiday cycle event around the greater Yellowstone area. It doesn't actually go in the park but sounded amazing with camp sites set up for you and even a beer truck coming along for the ride. Yet another reason to come back here if I didn't have enough already. That evening I was so tired I forgot to say anything interesting in my vlog and looked rather haggard and sunburnt. No time to put sun cream on when grasshoppers were about! I had little red arrow shapes burnt on my forehead from the slits in my helmet. Quite a comedy look that was first billing in the nightly vlog!

DAY 14:
JOLIET TO HARDIN

My jersey pockets were again stuffed full of lovingly made snack packs of eggs, cucumbers and tomatoes on my departure. Another sad wave goodbye as I ripped the band aid off and got going en route to the largest city in Montana, Billings. Cycling next to the train track just out of town, I spied a lady in the distance waving and shouting at me very enthusiastically. What's the panic, was there someone on the tracks? Has there been an accident? As I got closer my concern changed to laughter as I realised it was one of my new cycling friends from the night before. She had been tipped off I was en route and had come out to cheer me on! I was thrilled that someone in the middle of nowhere knew my name and had actually made the effort to come and wave me on. I stopped for a happy hug and chat, thinking for a moment I was on my own 'Tour de Gem' race across the country. It put the biggest smile on my face for the rest of the morning.

I was now in the habit of planning which shop I would stop at. Firstly, to be efficient and avoid cycling around wondering what was ahead, and secondly, as when I find a store with a coffee and food option I like it becomes my "go to" home from home. As boring as it seems, it was a joy in my day to be somewhere 'familiar', and a gas station called 'Town Pump' was my new favourite. The city of Billings was nothing to write home about and neither was the cycle. Looking up the final 50 miles from Billings to Hardin on my phone, it seemingly had nothing at all along the route. So I bought some supplies, filled up all 3 water bottles and headed out into the blazing sun and 50 miles of cycling that I will never forget.

The road into nowhere had no tree cover at all, no vehicles and a view for miles in each direction. It was peaceful, beautiful, and with no objects to gauge distance and size of the surroundings, my mind was playing tricks on me. Alongside the heat, causing wet-look mirages on the road, I was constantly questioning what I was seeing. I may or may not have seen an eagle, meerkats were running around at the side of the road, (which is a strange sight out of Africa), and there seemed to be twisters in the fields. I think I might have been hallucinating in the crazy heat. I finally dived out of the heat at the motel in Hardin, completing the days 85 miles before 2pm, my fastest day on paper so far. I wanted to carry on, but with no other stopping option for the next 65 miles it was an enforced early finish. An afternoon of chilling ensued, doing all the usual bike and route chores. I found an antidote to my painful dry and cracked lips from the local drug store, and told myself I needed to up my suncream stops over the next few days. To help out I had taken to wearing my buff over my face for the hottest parts of the day along with my jacket. The uncomfortable heat was a far better choice than being burnt as my factor 100 sweated off. On the plus side, I did find out that it may have been an eagle I saw, the meerkats were 'prairie dogs', and the twisters were definitely 'dirt devils'. I also now had my own pet grasshopper after mistakenly kidnapping from the previous day. Or was it a cricket I was chasing around the room? Lots of wasted Google time on that one!

This town was on the eastern side of a 'reservation' area, one of multiple that reside in this part of the USA. These areas were 'given' to the native people to live on after they were 'taken' by the 'white people' approximately 100 years ago. Seemed like the truth left behind from the Wild West stories depicted in many a film. Clearly a part of history that the country tries to hide! Can you give land back to someone you took it from? Either way, I'm sure I would find out more along the way, as I would be going in and out of various reservations in Wyoming and South Dakota over the next couple of days. It was recommended not to hang around or stay in these areas by anyone I had met so far. This made accommodation options scarce, and route planning difficult to know what to do for the best. It would be an interesting adventure, and a cultural history lesson about this seemingly forgotten part of US history.

DAY 15:
HARDIN TO SHERIDAN

I got an early start with the prospect of a day of frontage roads (old highway), following the I90 route all the way to Sheridan. Some 16 miles out of town was the 'Little Bighorn' battlefield monument. I was hoping I could get a peak at even though it was hours until it opened, but unfortunately no luck with large entrance gates stopping the view. The battle of Little Bighorn was where General Custer made 'his last stand' as it is now known. I won't go into detail on here but in short, Custer's army lost the battle against the native Indians all perishing in the battle. It's a controversial story depending on which side you read it from, with this monument's narrative dedicated to the 'loser' of the battle. How strange? Maybe I would have been more educated on the situation should I have properly visited, but history generally only remembers and celebrates the winners, or the 'good' over the 'bad'. Earlier I had cycled passed the newly erected memorial to all the native Indians who died in the many battles during this era. Safe to say it was a provocative part of history that was now coming to the forefront with efforts for a 'fairer' narrative to be represented. The reservations were the real life outcome from these times, and made me a little apprehensive of what to expect.

On entering some of the small towns in the 'Crow' reservation, the deprivation and evident poverty made me both sad and angry. I stopped at the local supermarket housed in a large corrugated structure with only a small sign depicting it from identical farm buildings either side. The lady serving was lovely and asked where I was from and where I was going to. We had a small conversation and when nobody else was looking she took my arm and said 'you know you are on reservation land?'. I replied I did and tried to seem positive about what I took as a quiet warning to be careful. I wished her well and sat down to eat at a makeshift table where an older gentleman asking the usual questions quickly joined me. He was hard of hearing and our different accents and language made conversation near impossible. He pursued in trying to converse, and at one point took to feeling my bicep and leg muscle saying 'strong' multiple times. He meant no harm so I tried not to visually protest to being prodded. He spoke of never having left the reservation, and I didn't really know what to say for the best, whilst I got smatterings of detail about the drilling in the area by the state, who keep the oil profits for themselves. Seemingly, the natives could live on the land but did not own it, or anything beneath it. I don't know if this was true or whether he thought I might be able to do something, or was merely telling a tale and making conversation. It was my second slightly uncomfortable conversation of the last 20 minutes. Clearly I was in a different world and couldn't pretend otherwise. I stuck out like a sore thumb and was clearly well off enough to fly to another part of the world and cycle through without question. I wished at times like these I could be a bit more inconspicuous and pretend to fit in, but that would be hypocritical at best.

I thought about these issues constantly over the next days, wondering what I would think if I lived in the area, and only coming up with more questions. I was just passing through and my little trip wasn't going to change anything about this situation; acting with kindness and trust to everyone seemed to be best I could do. I'm sure being a female tourist helped in being continuously well received, which I was so grateful for.

The boring road continued on and on and whilst I zoned out to the world, lost in my headphones, suddenly the road in front of me turn into a river. I couldn't believe I had missed this; I was always meticulous at checking the route the night before several times and memorising all the details. Checking the map my little blue dot was indeed by the river at the end of the road. The crossover point to the opposite I90 frontage road was 3 miles back. I could see the road the other side of the not very busy highway and decided to cross. Standing in my way was a small chest height reasonably flimsy barred wire fence, and I assumed the same the other side. I could easily get my bike over it and probably myself with no repercussions. I removed some of the bags when I started thinking about telling the story of jumping a barred wire fence and running across the highway as part of my daily tale. Surely just another funny story to add to the trip? Or a tale of cuts, bruises, ripped clothes and playing chicken with the trucks? We will never know as I clipped the bags back on and started the 6 mile correction. I stayed annoyed at myself for far too long, and not helped by the mundane ride I had got in the habit of focussing on faster efficient miles in the morning with carefully planned stops, so I had broken the back of the mileage when the heat came. Mistakes like this were just not acceptable I told myself and needed to do better. A bit over the top with the benefit of hindsight, but the big miles were starting to hurt!

In the afternoon I crossed over the boarder to Wyoming, also marking the end of the reservation. I got the obligatory picture helped by a lady from the nearby ranch, then carried onto the next town of Rochester. The delightful café I had picked out was a million miles away from the afternoon's scenery. The baristas asked if I had cycled through the reservation and whether I had any problems. I was pleased to announce that everyone I met was lovely and they were glad to hear it. The day finished in the city of Sheridan, which looked like a significant place on the map, however has a population equivalent to the towns of Chertsey or Addlestone near me, highlighting this 'least populous' US state. It was the perfect size having everything you need and nothing you don't, with the usual easy to navigate grid system. I already knew my host was going to be lovely as was the tradition now. Jen was a little younger than myself, super chatty and just the right amount of crazy! Whilst out for pizza I decided to get some clarity on whether my 'Wyoming facts' provided by friends back home were true. So... Fact 1: Wyoming is nicknamed the 'equality state', the first to allow women to vote, and the first to have a female governor. 'So it's a forward thinking state' I asked in hopeful anticipation. 'Are you kidding? Wyoming would let a sheep vote if they could!' came the reply. I didn't need any more facts after this, and a night of interesting conversation followed. As already mentioned, Wyoming is the least populous state in the USA by area, and joint last in the College Electorate ranking system with only 3 points. By comparison the state with the most points is California with 55. You'll be pleased to know I'm not going to go into detail about how the USA political system works, but in short this means states like Wyoming do not hold any clout in elections, and their vote is seen as unimportant, hence the sheep voting comment. If women or animals can vote, their voting population is greater, therefore possibly giving them more clout etc. On further research, the reasons for the 'equity state' nickname are varied, although it would seem irrelevant anyway as the State is far from equal for women. The current ranking of women's equality in terms of pay and education gaps etc, all present Wyoming in the bottom 5 of the USA. Jen, a child psychologist in training was even planning on moving out of the state to a more 'reasonable' one due to the political climate and culture. Such a good inside view of life out here, that I would never have if I had stopped in motels every night. I would have to give up these luxuries for a while and do some research as hosts were getting scarce and I would have to rely on motels for a while.

DAY 16:
SHERIDAN TO GILLETTE

In order to avoid the I90, I followed route 14 all the way to Gillette over the hills. I was a bit apprehensive as there was a gas station 42 miles away, which I could make with enough water, but after that there didn't seem to be anything. Once en route these feelings of apprehension disappeared. Unlike the crazy mirage road of a few days ago, there were many farms on this beautiful road which I could always duck into for water if necessary. It turned out once I had reached the gas station, there was a bar 32 miles ahead. The aptly named 'Spotted Horse' bar turned out to be the only thing in the town of 'Spotted Horse' with a population of two. So very random, I loved it but they didn't seem to like me so much as I didn't want a beer or food and only to refill my bottles. I didn't know if the lady was joking when she said there was a charge for water, a bit of an awkward interaction! The bar was definitely a bikers' stop; where I talked to a nice couple who couldn't believe and understand why I was cycling all this way in the heat. In turn, I did not understand why they didn't wear helmets or any protective clothing on their gas guzzling Harley Davidsons, and a lively happy debate arose. They were on their way to the world-famous Sturgis rally a couple of hundred miles the other side of the Black Hills in South Dakota. I knew about this 'mecca for bikers' and had slightly re-routed to avoid the event. I was seeing more bikers each day en route, riding the most lavish 'car sized' bikes. Even if you don't like bikes you can't help but be impressed with these machines and could hear them coming from miles off, especially in the stillness of the countryside. I spent a lot of the day getting as many waves and honks of their horns as I could, it was excellent daily entertainment. I could see why they detoured to this route rather than the highway, it was no brainer really, with over 100 miles of beautiful rolling hills, with scenery to match Montana in places. If this was back home it would have been a must do 'century ride' packed with weekend cyclists. So strange it was just me and the bikers all day, nonetheless I decided to treat it like a training ride constantly doing 'bike maths' the whole way calculating the elevation and speeds that I needed to do to for a consistent ride. It was rather painful at times and had to do some extra stops to get rid of 'cyclist hot foot' and apply extra sun cream. All in all I was so chuffed once I reached Gillette having completed 111 miles and over 3600 feet of climbing with a good average. It was the longest mileage I had ever done in a day and the discipline on the bike had paid off, setting me up for some long days ahead.

DAY 17:
GILETTE TO NEWCASTLE

I didn't relish getting up early this morning being so tired from the day before. My hosts had left breakfast out for me and I happily ate a few bowls of cereal. I didn't want to leave without saying goodbye and heard them getting up as I was just finishing. We had a cup of coffee and a chat before I left and still managed to make it out the door by 07.30. I had been trying to figure out for a while how to get to the 'Devils Tower' the main site in the area. The 'tower' is a large rock protruding over 1000 feet, and famous for its use in the Spielberg film 'Close Encounters Of The Third Kind'. I was 'passing by' in USA terms, which in real terms meant detouring 30 miles up a road and back, adding 60 miles to the day. I was looking into maybe going part way so I could see it from afar before turning back, or getting a taxi for that part. In the end it just seemed silly thinking I might add this mileage to my day, I felt I had already seen it in so many pictures and therefore ditched the idea. I would have to pass it by and wave at the sign just like Yellowstone.

Once that mileage was taken out, today seemed a relatively short and easy 75 miles in comparison with the day before. Once on the road, this optimism and naivety was quickly blown away after the first 10 miles. I was cycling through a massive headwind and my usual positivity was waning. The bike was being blown all over the place, and it was depressing to see how long it was taking me to do each mile. It was painful cycling trying to make the bike move, with my feet and arms aching in the relentless wind. The scenery had suddenly changed to boring oversize industrial, and unfortunately, I couldn't hear anything in my headphones over the wind and just had to get my head down and get on with it.

About 15 miles from Newcastle, I saw a row of trees and hid from the wind for a while, cheering myself up by finishing a packet of non-exciting biscuits. I just wanted to collapse behind these trees and not move until the wind changed direction. I knew a storm was closing in and needed to race to Newcastle before it hit. It felt like the slowest race ever at less than 10 mph but I finally made the motel and happily stopped. All thoughts of missing the Devils Tower had long since passed, this day was hard enough already. Twenty minutes after arriving, I watched the epic storm pass over creating rivers down the road and shaking the building with the deafening thunder. I hunkered down with some plastic cheese and crackers from the local gas station and watched back-to-back episodes of Downton Abbey. If you ignored the ads every five minutes and the poor excuse for cheese, I could have been at home, and it was a very comforting indeed.

Tomorrow was a huge day with big miles and even bigger hills, but encouraged by my new favourite website 'WillyWeather.com', the weather was going to improve. Alongside detailing the rain, it showed the wind direction at different times of the day and tomorrow was mainly a tail wind and far less severe if a headwind. I had the feeling this website would be my new best friend in the coming weeks, I didn't want to end up in my own version of the 90's film 'Twister', although I'm sure that would make a great evening vlog, or at least more exciting than talking about cheese as the day's highlight!

DAY 18:
NEWCASTLE
TO RAPID CITY

U p and out by 05.20 excited to get stuck into my monster day of heading into the Black Hills, en route to Mount Rushmore. My favourite time of the day to cycle watching the sun come up in the stillness never seemed to gets boring. I passed into South Dakota in the twilight on my way to the town of Custer. I made the 40 miles in 3 hours arriving about 8.30 in time for second breakfast. It was a lovely place and I got talking to a family on a nearby table whilst enjoying my stack of pancakes. The dad had always wanted to cycle across the USA, which gave me the go ahead to brashly drag my table over for an extended chit chat. By the time I had to leave, I think I had convinced him that it was a great idea, and the family seemed surprisingly super supportive. I happily left Custer a lot later than I planned, following many positive interactions in the local supermarket, and made my way to the 'Crazy Horse' memorial. This is the Native American equivalent of Mount Rushmore with a sculpture of the famous leader 'Crazy Horse' carved into the mountain. He was one of the victors in battle of Little Bighorn, and as there are no photos of him the memorial is more symbolic to the Native Americans as a whole. It was started in 1948 and is far from being finished with only the head and part of his outstretched arm complete. When it is completed it will dwarf the presidential faces on Mount Rushmore 17 miles up the road.

It was an interesting and worthwhile stop before starting those 17 miles. I was in such a happy mood en route in these breathtaking hills, and to think that I originally routed round them more a flatter route seemed mad! I did not know what to expect from this area, but it had exceeded whatever they were and I was in my element. There were plenty of up and downs but no big passes. As soon as I was knackered on the ups, the downs would appear with enough momentum to get a least halfway up the next one. It was a cyclist's playground and just a shame I was the only one out to play. It was like a rocket had been lit behind me, no energy conservation was happening today, I was having far too much fun!

Mount Rushmore soon came, and I was prepared to be disappointed as per the reviews. The statues were indeed very small and disappointing, good job they were in a beautiful place to make the journey worth it. As expected with all 'must see' tourists traps, the monument was dwarfed by the vast complex of hotels, restaurants, and general tat. I didn't stay long and was back on the road headed towards Rapid City, or so I thought. After a while I realised the sat nav was taking me towards a mountain bike trail that wouldn't be suitable and had to back track several miles over the hills. Never mind, at least I saw the funny side this time and tried to enjoy it. The only rubbish part of the day was passing through Rapid City to my hosts on the opposite side. This slog was easily forgotten at arrival to their stunning self-built house overlooking a beautiful valley. I had landed on my feet yet again and was so happy with one of my best days 'on paper' to rival the cascades pass on day 3. My elevation totalled 7000 feet over 94 miles, and I had such a super time doing it. Fabulous scenery, great roads, a positive focus, and calm weather were a recipe for good day.

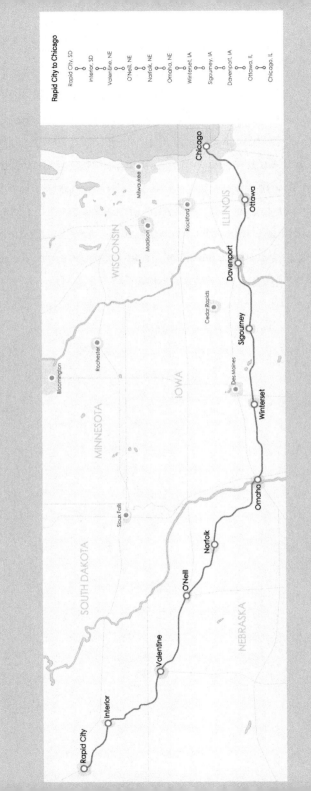

Rapid City to Chicago

Rapid City, SD
Interior, SD
Valentine, NE
O'Neill, NE
Norfolk, NE
Omaha, NE
Winterset, IA
Sigourney, IA
Davenport, IA
Ottawa, IL
Chicago, IL

PART
4
THROUGH THE PLAINS

DAY 19:
RAPID CITY TO INTERIOR

I wasn't looking forward to fighting my way out of Rapid City in the morning, but my host showed me a bike route through beside a river. It was slow but pretty and a welcome start as I attempted to wake up on the bike. Today I was heading towards the 'Badlands' National Park, and didn't really twig how long it would be before I made it there. In hindsight this was an 'ignorance is bliss' moment, with boring undulating roads and another 25 mile boiling stint on the interstate, it was another 'head down and crack on' kind of a day. When I finally made the park gates at mile 75 I wasn't really in the mood for sightseeing and was rather spent. I attempted to enjoy the 24 mile ride through to the town of Interior at the opposite end. It was a rocky and barren landscape that resembled a scene from Mars or a mini Grand Canyon and was luckily predominantly downhill. I enjoyed the winding roads snaking through, stopping for a trail and a picture here and there. It was not uninteresting at all and definitely worth a visit if you are in the area, but with the combination of wanting to finish my day asap, and the luxury of having visited places like the Grand Canyon before, I didn't stop that much and wanted to press on. I did come across many more prairie dogs for a bit of extra entertainment along the way.

It wasn't difficult to find the only motel in Interior, along with the one bar that served food. The local shop had no fresh food, and only enough amenities in the town for its population of 94! I was glad to be too tired to want to wander around and explore, spending the evening planning the next day. I had a choice of carrying on through South Dakota or down through Nebraska on a rough line to Chicago. The road through Nebraska was the obvious choice with more accommodation options as well as being much flatter. The tricky part was how to make it down there from here with nothing for well over 100 miles, and zigzagging south west along the grid system. I knew many of the roads would be gravel and with limited 'Google street view' to check, it was going to be a bit 'pot luck'. Before an early night, I made the best mini map of route options that I could and stuck it to my bike. Along with an expected headwind, probable rain and possible thunderstorms, I had set my alarm for 04.30am.

DAY 20:
INTERIOR TO VALENTINE

A day I'll never forget....
On the road at 5 in time to watch a beautiful sunrise. I got this one on video along with one of my favourite pictures of the trip that could only be captured at the right time of day. My cycling shadow against the bright yellow maize field that went all the way to the horizon. It took a few attempts to get the perfect angle but what a picture to remember this part of the world. Soon after this, my photography efforts turned to capturing the lightning forks coming from the approaching storm. The contrast of the bright sky ahead and the dark clouds behind against this landscape really was quite an amazing sight. I would have enjoyed watching it more if I had not been on my bike and it wasn't heading straight for me. There was no way I could avoid it and hoped that there would be somewhere I could shelter ahead. Eventually it caught up with me and I cycled on looking for shelter. Now, I'm sure we have all been in a rainstorm before,

but I have never experienced anything like this ever! The hailstones were painful, I could hardly see, the road had turned into a river, and as soon as the lightning stated coming down in the surrounding fields I dived into a nearby property desperate for cover. The barn was locked and the only shelter was a slightly overhanging roof from a mobile home with barely enough room to cover my bike. This took precedent over me with much needed resources to keep dry, my waterproof bags would be no match for this storm. I spied the open window of a truck and assuming it was unlocked I ran over and got in. I felt awful hiding out in a random truck without asking but was definitely 'sorry not sorry' in my desperation. After about 10 minutes my luck ran out as the house owner stood staring at me from the doorway.

'Damn it' I thought, I'd just been busted sitting in his car. I quickly leapt out running over shouting many apologise. As I got closer it was obvious that he had physical and mental difficulties, and I hoped that my reason for being in his car was obvious and he could understand me. He didn't communicate anything and eventually headed back to a room beyond the living room leaving the door open. I had no idea what was happening and what to say, but there was now space inside the doorway to shelter in and I took the opportunity. I stood there for a while wondering what to do before a lady came out, who I assumed was his wife, and started talking at me. I had no idea what she was saying, so kept apologising for the intrusion saying I was trying to get out of the rain. She then walked over to the window opened the curtain and looked out as if to decide what the weather was doing. 'How do you not know it's a storm?' I thought, it couldn't be more obvious. They could have been forgiven a little for not hearing the noise over the massive blaring TV in the corner but still, really? She left as quickly as she came and a few minutes later a teenage girl appeared with some car keys. I said 'hello' and she replied the same with a smile before going outside to lock the car. 'I'm not going to steal your car' I thought but probably best practice to keep these things locked up. She also returned to the back of the house and over the next 20 minutes many other teenagers appeared going back and forth from what I assumed was the bathroom. This was just the most bizarre situation as I stood inside the doorway watching (now joined by my bike), in the early hours, and wearing day glow clothing illuminating the room with flashing bike lights. I must have looked like an alien from outer space to them. Whilst trying and failing to be inconspicuous the decor of the room just hit me as I took in the scene. The smell of stale smoke and beer cans strewn everywhere was quite overwhelming, with a variety of taxidermy exhibited around the walls and the carpet and boards merging into one. I suddenly came to my senses as the storm died down and thought 'what am I doing?', 'this is not the place to be'. I grabbed my bike and rode out as quickly as I could.

Once out of view of the house I felt both relieved to be out of the storm and the house; awkward to the max! The road I had just turned onto was soaking wet gravel and a complete no go. My wheels had carved a nice groove in the road, there was no hiding where I had been! I consulted the soggy map stuck to my bars and had a think. This road was the straightest way and would hopefully dry up before long, but I'd had my fill of surprises for one day. I just had to suck up the fact that, instead of zigzagging from one corner of a rectangle to the other, I would have to take the longer way around the outside. At least I would be certain of tarmac if nothing else. The next 'place' on the map was a store 15 miles away and I reluctantly backtracked in its direction shivering uncontrollably on the bike. I probably should have changed into dry clothes, but the saturated wet ones had nowhere to go without making everything else wet, they would dry quicker on me.

An hour later I landed at the store in Wanblee and sat hiding in the corner eating, trying to keep myself to myself. Eventually a local asked about where I was going and I took the opportunity to ask about my route. I still had options of going through the middle, but he wasn't sure whether the roads were fully tarmacked. If a local didn't know these roads, then I wasn't going to chance it. Decision made, I was heading the long way round in the direction of White River 46 miles away.

One thing keeping me on my toes on the way out of town was running the 'scary dog gauntlet'. This game involved trying to get level to the houses before they leapt up from the yards barking & snarling and chasing me up the road. These dogs were not my friends, and it got way too close for comfort a few times nearly kicking a few away. I was pleased to get rid of the dogs out of town just as the temperature started to rise. There is always a lovely optimum hour in the day of the perfect cycling temperature, then suddenly my energy is zapped instantly and it's constant layers of sun cream, or covering up. Knowing that I wouldn't want to re-start after each sunscreen stop, I chose a day for covering up instead.

The road surface had not been good so far and was now beginning to get frustrating. No tarmac here - just concrete slabs butted up to each other with tar in the gaps. Most of the tar had long since deteriorated leaving cracks and channels across the road evenly spaced. This was hard going, having to be on constant watch with brakes at the ready as I slalomed all over the road. It didn't take long before the inevitable happened and I heard my back tyre puncture. 'Keep it coming' I thought as I dismantled the bike, 'what else can you throw at me today?' I'd just about had enough and after a tricky and time-consuming puncture, I was melting in the heat, and a stop was needed. I found a tree where, if I curled my legs in and didn't move, there was just enough shade, hurrah!

This day was just going to be long and it really didn't matter how long it took. I was in a motel with no hosts waiting for me, and the time it took was irrelevant, 'I'll just keep pedalling', I thought, and I will make it in the end. I cheered up a little after letting go of the frustrations as I headed towards White River. I entertained myself along the way by guessing how far ahead the 'object' on the horizon was. This usually took the form of a large farm building or grain store, and I was getting pretty good at estimating distances. Sounds very boring but kept my mind busy and the miles rolling by.

I made White River and stopped at the nearest gas station celebrating with a large ice-cold fizzy drink. I hid in the shade around the back of the gas station, as I really didn't want to talk to anyone today and if I could smell myself it must be bad! The next pit stop was 'Mission' 25 miles away and was hard to get motivated to move. I had hoped that the new road I'd just joined would be in better condition, but sadly it was not. This busier road with increased traffic made slaloming around the cracks difficult, and the slow depressing slog continued. About 10 miles further on a huge set of roadworks appeared. I thought I was going slow already but I was now on dirt, attempting to dodge the worst parts, whilst being aware of the trucks coming in both directions. The sections were so long that traffic was coming back and forth as I made my way through. Although frustrating, a new distraction and at least the road was getting fixed!

I was happy to finally arrive at the supermarket and forage for some food. I didn't know the time and official miles as my Garmin had long since run out of battery. It was still capturing the data but hidden away in my bag plugged into my powerbank. The best place for it, nothing was more demoralising than staring at the mileage when you want to be off the bike. I was hoping for some hot food from the café but I had turned up too late and that part was closed. After munching on unhealthy food I started the last 31 miles to Valentine. It sounded like a lovely place, and at least it was flatter as I kept my eyes pealed for the 'Nebraska' sign. I don't remember anything about this part of the journey apart from knowing instantly when I had changed state. There was no sign, but the well-kept lawns and houses had returned, the nice road surface was back and it looked like I was riding in a different land.

I rolled into the motel at dusk with a sense of elation and the bonus of a nice motel room! After the best bath I've ever had and a much-needed clothes washing session, I relaxed and took in the day. I added up all the distances saved which totalled a whooping 133 miles with over 4000 foot elevation. I knew today was going to be big but 133 was just epic and the furthest I had ever cycled in a day. A super achievement on any day, but adding in the storm, a puncture, awful roads, crazy heat and a random excursion into someone's car and house, I had a lot to be pleased about, and sent home the longest video blog of the trip. It ended 'whatever happens tomorrow it just has to be a better day, right?' I went to bed feeling like I could take on the world again tomorrow, hoping my body would be up to the task!

DAY 21:
INTERIOR
TO O'NEILL

A huge storm had woken me up several times in the night and I walked into breakfast bleary eyed. I wasn't expecting anything wildly exciting, but the amount of plastic waste on offer was something else. All the bowls, cups and cutlery etc were made of polystyrene with every slice of bread and premade mini omelettes individually wrapped in a plastic bag. I staged a pointless one woman protest to all this, washing my bowl and cup between different items and using my trusty spork. Before leaving I even washed up my bowl and cup and placed it back on the pile, I just couldn't bear throwing it in the bin!

I turned out of the motel straight into a head wind and my 'take on the world' attitude died an instant death. I ended up having to do this first bit twice after backtracking to retrieve my water bottles left in the fridge. Today I was following Highway 20 for the whole day which ran parallel to the 'cowboy' cycle trail.

Originally, I had planned to cycle this route as I assumed if there was an official cycle route then there must be facilities and something to see. It turned out the cycle route was mostly gravel and had not been maintained since created, as most cycling routes are. Funding can usually be found for 'green transport' options, but no one wants to fund ongoing upkeep. At least if I was following the same road all day I couldn't get lost, and as I hadn't booked ahead, would just see how far I got. Not being a tourist area, with towns sporting a motel every ten to twenty miles, I thought I'd try and go with the flow a little.

At mile 25 I was sat on a bench having a break, when a shout from behind of 'do you need some water or some ice?' broke my sleepy daze. I hadn't even noticed 'Grandma's Tea Room' before stopping, and this was evidently Grandma offering refreshments. A cup of tea would be amazing I thought, but zero chance of that and I replied 'do you have any coffee?' instead. She ushered me in and started boiling us up a pot. The cute shop was a million miles away from my random house excursion of yesterday with no taxidermy in sight only cute teddy bears, sewing crafts, and more doyley's than you could count! It looked like it was plucked right out of the English countryside and we had a lovely chat with an atlas to help out my story. Amazing how a chat, cup of coffee, and a map can perk up my day; my mood had completely changed as I left. The other thing that had changed was the wind moving 90 degrees to be a side wind! I quickly checked in with 'Willy Weather' to see it would be turning all day and also dying down. These lovely intereactions carried on all day with the lady in front of me paying for my morning snacks, and a lovely trucker paying for my sandwich at lunch time. He had seen me several times today on his errands and I was so touched by my Nebraskan welcome. I had yet to open my wallet and everyone was so lovely and welcoming.

I stopped at every main town along my slow plod of a day with a coffee here, and an ice-cream there to keep me going. I hardly spent anything all day and felt kind watchful eyes looking out for me on the road with smiles and waves. Due to a 'no room at the inn situation' at my desired stop, I reluctantly cycled the extra 25 miles to the next town resulting in a surprising daily total of 112 miles. A brilliant start to Nebraska, and couldn't have been more different to the previous day.

DAY 22:
O'NEILL TO NORFOLK

As was now the norm I woke up super tired, this time due to a late night of bike maintenance. It was my own fault for tweaking my creaking bike and turning a screw the wrong way. Loosening a screw with my very small bike tool was no problem, but just too short and bulky to get enough torque to tighten it up again, and after hours of trying I had given up. I now didn't have the large front ring in use, but it was still rideable so not a disaster. I would stop at a local garage to borrow a screwdriver on route. As it happens, I saw a cutlery knife in the deserted lobby and fix it in about 10 seconds. Annoyed I had stayed up late wasting my time when all I needed was a cutlery knife! Maybe this should be a must have along with the emergency cable ties and duck tape!

Once on the road I was looking forward to seeing if the Nebraska loveliness continued, and as soon as I entered the first gas station a group of 3 ladies started talking to me. Before I knew it, I was sat down with a hot chocolate in hand joining in with their coffee morning! Once the usual questions were finished, one said it was a shame her friend Louanne couldn't join them today as she wrote for the local paper and would love the story. Very quickly Louanne was phoned and would meet me at the next gas station 10 miles up the road. I knew I had absolutely no choice in this whatsoever and was amused greatly. True to their word, when I arrived at the next gas station Louanne was waiting with a clip board in hand. I got the impression it was a very local paper indeed and did my best at trying to make sure my name was spelt correctly and I was as animated as possible. Although 'Gemma' seems such a normal name to me, I always forget it does not really exist outside of the UK, and I generally got called Emma, which I never corrected. We had a lovely chat and I cycled off wondering if anything would come of 'Jenna Sitwells' journey across the USA!

It was then a 60 mile stint to a bike shop in Norfolk, and much like Norfolk in the UK it was flat. I should have been whizzing along, especially when the elevation measured in the low hundreds of feet rather than in the usual thousands, but alas the tiredness had caught up. A surprising hill appeared and zapped the last of my energy to the bike shop. Luckily there was no one else in the shop and my bike received a new chain and gear cables for the bargain price of £32.00. It would have cost the same just for the labour back home, another win for Nebraska! With the welcome rest I rang the motel in the next town which was unfortunately full. It would have to be an early stop here at

75miles. There were plenty of cheap places to stay on the busy ring road sandwiched between drive through restaurants and mini malls. The noise and traffic was a bit overwhelming and I didn't like it one bit, but the extra time and rest was much needed. I just couldn't help being disappointed that I had only made 75 miles on the flattest day so far, and would sleep off my frustration and crack on tomorrow.

DAY 23:
NORFOLK
TO OMAHA

With a decent sleep I headed out early en route to Omaha close to the state border. With a population of just under half a million it's the largest city in Nebraska. I had originally routed north of the city, but knowing how sparsely this part of the USA is I thought it best to stay 'close', in USA terms of course. I spent most of the day contemplating whether this was a good decision as it added on many miles that didn't need to be done. You never know whether your decision is the best and once made you just have to go with it, but today I couldn't shift the annoyance and lacked positivity. The rain and head wind didn't help - mirroring my rubbish mood. It was a hard going 104 miles with the never-ending corn fields. All this disappeared as usual on arrival at my host's house, and whilst being taken out to her friend's birthday party for the evening, I was reflecting on my time in the state.

That morning as I walked up to the cashier to pay for my drink, she announced a new policy to everyone of 'free hot chocolates for people who cycle in the rain!'. It took me far too long to gauge that clearly this wasn't the standard policy and she was just being super nice. I managed to style this out and give her a very wet hug as a lame exchange. The kindness of strangers in this state was rather overwhelming at times and is an amazing example of the difference a bit of kindness makes to your day. It might have been visitor's luck that I was greeted in this way, but I got the impression that it's standard practice in these close-knit communities. I would have fond memories of the people and the state, and hoped the vibe would carry on in Iowa when I crossed the Missouri in the morning.

DAY 24:
OMAHA TO WINTERSET

alf of me wondered what the day in Iowa would bring, and due to technology the other half already knew. It would be hillier, rainy, with headwind and a view of corn fields. A bit deflated I set off wishing I hadn't checked so I could be in an adventurous and 'ignorance is bliss' kind of mood. I told myself I wouldn't bother checking the next days ahead, knowing that was already unlikely, it's just too tempting and normal procedure now.

The slog of a morning through the wind, rain and rolling hills was tricky, and I mentally picked off the small towns one by one whilst listening to some tunes. Definitely not a day for looking at the miles and hid my Garmin away. The afternoon's weather perked up a bit with occasional sunshine and new animal sightings. Plenty of birds of prey swooping past, racoon roadkill, and hundreds of frazzled frogs creating a fun slalom. I had an 'eye-spy' list from my friends informing me of fun Iowa facts. I was keeping my eyes peeled for pigs as these out populate people in the state by four to one, and John Wayne Iowa's famous Alumni. No luck with the pigs but did pass the John Wayne museum in my hosts town of Winterset so a win for that one. My instructions were to go to the supermarket then ring for a lift. I always enjoy a pick up ride and Rich and his dog were a welcome sight as we headed back to his house complete with chickens, and a barn the size of an aircraft hanger, easily dwarfing the house. Rich was bike mad with custom built eccentric bikes in all shapes and sizes filling his barn, along with many other on the go projects. We had a great evening filled with yummy food, lively debate and talk of the 'Bridges of Madison County'. I hadn't seen the film, and had no idea I was in 'The' Madison County, with the famous bridges just up the road. How did this miss my eye spy list? I would be getting a personal tour in the morning to find out more before heading back to the supermarket.

DAY 25:
WINTERSET TO SIGOURNEY

W ith chickens for an early alarm clock, I came downstairs to Rich cooking me a wonderful breakfast. We ate and chatted for an hour about all things usually avoided with strangers; Religion, politics, ideologies and all the ins and outs of Brexit, as it was before I left anyway. I then got my personal tour of the famous bridges that Rich helps to manage, reading the visitor blogs and being a tourist for a while before heading back into town. It was already a later than usual start, but on pulling up to the supermarket, there was no getting away quickly as I was requested to meet his friends for a coffee. He knew me well already, knowing that I wouldn't resist a coffee morning ushering me over to a large group of about 20 people. Before I could take in all the smiling faces and say 'hello', a chair appeared, coffee was poured and questions came from all directions. I was in my element and felt very loved indeed. What an excellent community and a shame I couldn't stay another day. I had offers for dinner, various trips out and even a round of golf! I could have stayed all day chatting, but as ever the time was ticking and I dragged myself away against my better wishes. I cycled off upbeat and loving life, twinned with the sadness of leaving my new friends - so strange after being in town for only 15 hours. I wondered if I would ever pass this way again, and these thoughts took up much of my thinking for the day. I would love to say there was a lot to see, but unless you love corn fields and massive machinery it was much like the days before, nevertheless a comforting normal sight. There wasn't even any crazy weather, leaving a lack of things to report on in my daily vlog. I was one hundred per cent content with a boring day. It was quickly becoming difficult enough just to push the bike through another 100 miles, no dramas needed.

I arrived at my host's around 18.30 and was welcomed with a lovely dinner. He was a keen cyclist and told me about riding the 'RAGBRAI' a couple of weeks before. It is an unnecessarily complicated acronym with the last four letters standing for 'Bicycle Ride Across Iowa'. The first three stand for 'Register's Annual Great' which doesn't exactly roll off the tongue. I was already clued up on this multiday cycling event that crosses the state, as Rich helped organise one of the sections. It sounded mad with approximately 8500 'official' riders in the event being dwarfed by the unofficial riders joining in randomly – and why not? People camped or slept wherever they could, cycled all kinds of bikes in this week long 'party cycle' that took over every town along the way. The UK could never get away with something like that. People get irate about organised rides with official road closures. Could you imagine party cyclists blocking the roads for a week and locals loving it? I know I would love it, so maybe I do need to come back out here and join in! After this lovely chat, an early night ensued with the mistake of checking the morning's weather. A massive thunderstorm was on its way. Why did I have to check that weather app!

DAY 26:
SIGOURNEY TO DAVENPORT

I left early in the dark hoping I could make some progress before the thunderstorm hit. My host was a bit worried about this situation and offered to give me lift part way, which was always an appreciated gesture, but not to be. About 30 minutes into the cycle, the storm started to hit, with warm rain, before the skies lit up with lightning. I carried on as best as I could, but it quickly became unsafe as I was blown off the road whilst managing 5mph. I had visions of hiding out in cars and strange houses, but found a respectable porch in a farmyard near a gift shop. There were chickens, goats and finally the elusive pigs running around that I had been keeping my eyes peeled for. To my left, a lady ran out the gift shop throwing a towel at me shouting that I could hide in the barn, before running back for cover. I spent the next 45 minutes having a lovely snooze on the seat of a massive tractor!

When the coast was clearer, I carried on up the road watching the storm, which was now ahead of me. I've never seen so many lightning forks, I was completely memorized by the scene all the way until Washington. Not 'The' Washington of course, but the one for today. I picked up some WIFI in a café and read messages from my host checking if I was still alive! He had sent some pictures copied from the news of overturned trucks on the interstate running parallel to my route. It felt great that I was being looked out for and he enjoyed my story of hiding out with the tractor and pigs.

The afternoon was full of the usual corn fields and very small towns. I had now got use to the corn fields being excellent cover for going to the toilet. No more waiting for cars to pass and nearly getting caught! Another bonus feature were the water towers in the centre of each town, easily visible from miles off. No chance of getting lost with these beacons every 10 miles or so, and easy targets to pick off along the way. I eventually came across a road closed sign and as usual went straight through hoping I could just wiggle around the problem. There was no such luck this time as the road descended into mud down a steep hill. After the storm there was no hope of even carrying my bike across, as I would easily be up to my knees in the mud. The detour added a couple of miles onto the day, but no big drama overall.

The sun appeared for the last section of the 104 mile day into Davenport, where I struggled the last 25, having lots of 'coke stops' to give me some sugar energy along the way. The cycling was theoretically easy and flat along the Mississippi, passing the biggest industrial factories I had ever seen. My host was waiting on the steps of his apartment, and shouted me over before I had even started to find the place. He lived above a shop in a room behind his signage workshop and was bike mad. He took me on a tour of the city he loved, where we ate pizza at one of his favourite bars and watched a big band play. Davenport was an industrial city with manufacturing at its core, and had a rough and ready look about it. My host was a little younger than me and loved people coming to stay and hearing about where they were from. Unfortunately, he didn't have the means to travel or a passport, and had rarely been out of the state. His outlet was people coming to stay with a visitors book full of comments from cyclists over the years. I hoped that one day he would have the means to live out his cycling dreams and travel over the USA. It was a much-needed reminder of how lucky I was to be doing this trip, and my gratefulness to all the kind hosts sharing parts of their worlds with me.

DAY 27:
DAVENPORT
TO OTTAWA

O ut early in search of food and the cycle tracks out of the city that my host loved. The first task was to cross the Mississippi into Illinois, with many impressive industrial bridges to choose from. Cycling through the outskirts was a double take of arriving here with at least 20 miles of giant industrial factories and run-down towns, eerily quiet so early in the morning. Further out I located the 'Hennepin Canal Parkway' which I planned to follow for most of the day. It was slow going but pleasant at first, before the track quickly deteriorated the further out of town I cycled. I needed to carry my bike on several occasions and felt I had persevered enough, before heading back to the road and the comfort of the cornfields.

There was nothing of note in the scenery today and I entertained myself by counting and mooing at the many uninterested cows. It was 5.30 by the time I rolled into the motel in Ottawa, now getting use to cycling for longer hours each day with increasing amounts of struggle and pain. I totted up the past 10 day total, and to my surprise it totalled 1025! Now not so surprising I was feeling the strain. Alongside accommodation reasons, I was pushing the miles with the hope of getting to Chicago one day ahead of the planned schedule. Thankfully I had succeeded in this target, praying I wouldn't have to pay the price in injury when I arrived. If you had asked me the day before, I would have been adamant about staying with the one planned rest day, keeping the bonus day in the bag, but today was a different matter. I wondered whether knowing I would make Chicago early made my mind relax giving my body permission to give up on me. All the same, I had changed my mind and was having two rest days, and couldn't wait to arrive tomorrow. For tonight, this upmarket commuter town was a reminder that I had completed the mid-west and was firmly back in city and suburban life.

DAY 28:
OTTAWA TO CHICAGO

I couldn't get up quickly enough today, wanting to speed through the 90 miles asap! This famous city had been on my hit list for years, and the possibility of two rest days was excellent motivation since starting this section in Missoula. I went as fast as I could through 70 miles of suburban towns and farms on the 'Illinois and Michigan' cycle trail, dodging the rain in various coffee shops en route. There was nothing of note, much like the last couple of days, but nothing not to like and I welcomed easy and enjoyable cycling. I took this in as much as I could before fighting the last 20 miles through the Southern Chicago Neighbourhoods with the downtown skyscrapers in the distance. This was some of the worst cycling I have ever done and nothing I want to repeat. The crazy traffic seemed to be aiming for me, with constant horn-honking and awful road conditions. I just pretended all the honking was a friendly 'hello' as I got my head down and got on with it.

If you have never been to downtown Chicago, it really is quite something. A plethora of architectural styles mixed up over the decades that actually seem to somehow blend together like no other city I have been to. I would even go as far as saying it was 'beautiful', which is quite surprising coming from a city escaper like me. To top it off, the picturesque lake, complete with miles of beaches, parks and perfectly separated running and cycling lanes ticked even more boxes. I knew I was going to have a great couple of days here after finding my hosts and getting some much-needed sleep.

I happily filled the days, enjoying cycling about without the bike bags, visiting museums, and all the usual touristy things including must do boat trips. It was a good job I had two days, as a migraine hit on the first and I spent a whole afternoon taking public snoozing to the next level, by adding in some public vomiting! Although it was rather lonesome being 'on holiday' by myself, it was an enjoyable couple of days in this fantastic city.

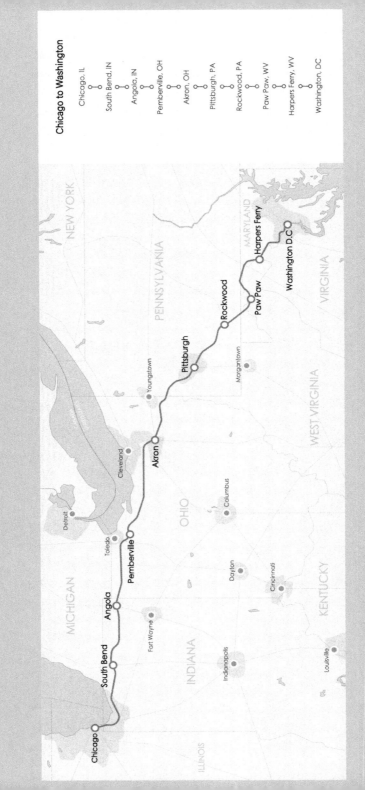

Chicago to Washington

Chicago, IL
South Bend, IN
Angola, IN
Pemberville, OH
Akron, OH
Pittsburgh, PA
Rockwood, PA
Paw Paw, WV
Harpers Ferry, WV
Washington, DC

PART
5
THE LAST LEG

DAY 29:
CHICAGO TO SOUTH BEND

I was raring to get the show back on the road this morning, leaving early. I had swapped hosts the night before, staying with an eccentric teacher who had also cycled across the country using the traditional route a couple of years before. She was animal mad, and I slept in her living room with the overly friendly cat, the uncaged cocker-too pooing everywhere, very much hoping the snake wasn't able to escape from its tank and join in the fun! All reasons to make me smile as I cycled along the beach front watching the sun come up.

I was soon into Indiana, a state that I had heard not so good things about, and had re-routed to avoid the cities. This was mainly to appease my friends because there had been more shootings than normal that made the UK headlines. For the first half of the day I followed bike lanes back through suburbia, then onto the familiar farmlands with a head wind. I had trouble finding a host in the area, and was heading to an 'Airbnb' on the outskirts of South Bend that looked easy to find. Just after I had booked this a host got back to me, and felt a bit sorry for myself that I was going to miss out on some chat that evening. The day had nothing of note much like the last couple of days, and was always going to be a not so interesting part of the ride. Due to the head wind, I turned up late, and then found out that I had gone through another time zone losing an hour. The Air BnB lady was a little annoyed at my tardy timekeeping, but I was paying for the room so I didn't feel that bad. I had 103 more miles in the bag and only 80 the next day.

DAY 30:
SOUTH BEND TO ANGOLA

I was so glad of this "shorter day" (which 80 miles seems to have become), as it was another boring and miserable one with a tough headwind and constant rain. With facilities now plentiful, I had plenty of coffee stops to dodge the rain as best as I could to keep my spirits up. In the late morning whilst watching the space in front of my wheel, I noticed the farm houses were looking quite well looked after and quaint, with picket fences, flower boxes and cute signs bearing the names of the owners. I didn't think much of this to begin with, until every farmhouse looked exactly the same. 'Wow people must really be proud of living here' I thought, maybe there was a competition for the best kept house or something. Strange that there was an 100% conformity rate to this look. It was as if I had time travelled back to 1950's America, with old school bikes, cars and carts dotted about. Whilst enjoying this strange world, I saw a horse drawn covered carriage coming towards me containing two ladies in blue dresses, driven by a man with a long beard. 'An Armish Community' I thought, and suddenly everything suddenly made sense. It was like cycling through the film set for 'Witness' with Harrison Ford. Everyone was so friendly waving back at me and I took it all in before the heavens opened. Luckily, I could see the bustling town centre containing exactly 3 stores at a crossroads ahead! One was a small restaurant selling the 'best pie in the county' and I flew in out of the rain as fast as I could.

The pie was indeed lovely and I enjoyed seeing the locals chat in their own language with a few 'outsiders' like myself enjoying the pie. There was no way to blend in here, and I felt awful about leaving a massive puddle on the floor which no amount cloths from the bathroom would clear. When the rain finally stopped I cycled back into this century for the last 25 miles of the day.

My hosts for the evening had a few businesses including the local bike shop where I met them and got a complementary bike check over. A great start to the evening in a Mexican restaurant, trip to the local ice-cream parlour, and brilliant conversation as always. They even had a piano with a Disney music book in the living room, what more could I want? Another day where I landed on my feet, feeling thankful for such welcoming hosts as the day's highlight. I was beginning to lack enthusiasm for much else and needed to do much better tomorrow!

DAY 31:
ANGOLA TO PEMBERVILLE

This bed was just so comfy it was like waking up in a hotel. Amazing what a good night's sleep can do, I felt reenergised to pass into Ohio today. Crossing off the states every couple of days was welcome motivation with the little scenery to look at. My friends back home were also helping my motivation by sending 'things to see in Ohio', as I scanned the map hoping some would be en route. Unfortunately, I would have to miss out on seeing the building shaped like a basket, but was genuinely sad not to be seeing the 'Ohio State Penitentiary', or as it's better known, the prison from the Shawshank Redemption. I'm sure it would just be disappointing in real life, or that's what I told myself anyway.

A couple of miles out of town I hit a double cycling jackpot, a significant tailwind twinned with a newly laid road of the most perfect tarmac I have ever seen. Who knew tarmac would be so utterly exciting, there was no time to lose and I raced along going as fast as I could manage. It was so exciting I even sent a video home explaining about the tarmac and wind duo, not apologising for my geeky sad moment, this news needed to be shared! There was no time for stopping, I ate on the bike with only quick stops to run into the corn fields for comfort breaks. I even chanced my luck ignoring several 'road closed' signs, waving at the unbothered contractors as they finished laying the road for me. Eventually the road came to an end, but 45 miles before 10.30am had me in high spirits. Where had this wind been through middle America!

Later in the day I had two memorable interactions. The first being a lady in a supermarket, who was most thrilled at spotting me sat on the floor. My 'lycra look' generally worked as a people repeller, but on this occasion bagged me chat about how there are no women cyclists in these parts apart from herself. She messaged me several times that day, and it was great to know that my little trip gave someone joy and helped the cause of cycling. Whilst speeding along and thinking of this, I spotted what looked to be a recumbent cyclist ahead. It took me a while to decide that's what it was, as the multiple bags attached everywhere made it the size of a small car. My first touring cyclist on the trip, this day was turning out to be a good one! In my excitement I cycled up alongside and shouted an enthusiastic 'Hello'. Clearly startled, he wobbled and came to a stop, looking rather bemused. 'Where are you going' I asked. 'Boston' he said looking displeased as I fired more questions at him trying to ease the tension. He eventually shouted 'what's with all the questions!', and I knew my time was up. I apologised for startling him, quickly making an awkward exit whilst wishing him well. Of all the people I had met on this trip, the most grumpy person just had to be a fellow cyclist! Maybe it was a good job I hadn't met many along the way.

I rolled into the cute town of Pemberville at 16:30 having completed the 93 miles in over a 16 mph average. My hosts were not back from work till after 18:00, so I hung out on their veranda happy with one of my best cycling days. Never underestimate the quality of the road surface and wind direction on a cyclist's happiness I thought, as I hoped for a repeat tomorrow!

DAY 32:
PEMBERVILLE TO AKRON

woke up super happy having got on like a house on fire with my new hosts. I had been taken out to dinner, looked after, educated about the local history, and even had a proper cup of tea from teapot! Tea bags would have been more than good enough, but I styled out using traditional tea leaves pretending this was the proper way of doing things. I wanted to stay more days here and was sad to leave.

This day was already going to be well over 100 miles, before adding the mistake of a wrong turn out of town. My new detour added at least 5 unnecessary miles, and I was so annoyed with myself I decided to stay on the highway rather than the country roads to make up these miles by way of punishment. There was nothing of note to see, so I got my head down and cracked onto the next point of interest, a 15 mile off road cycle route. Glad to mentally relax and be off the highway, I was slowly catching up with what looked like a racing tricycle ahead. I had not seen one of these before, it was clearly a home-made much-loved vehicle that only a cycling enthusiast would have. I got chatting to the owner who did indeed build the bike, complete with his name decaled on the top tube as many cyclists have. We zipped along at the same pace for over 10 miles engrossed in conversation. Once the route came to an end, he gave me directions back to the highway as he was ending here. It turned out he was due to stop 10 miles back where I had met him, but had carried on for a chat! What a top gent, totally made my day and reminded me how much the miles just whizzed by when you were having fun. Chatting, tail winds and proper tarmac were making up for the lack of motivational scenery in this area.

Now one positive to cycling over 100 miles a day, were 3 lunch stops rather than just the two. Or, second breakfast and double lunch…whichever looks slightly less greedy? It so happened that I realised I was missing my bike lock when stopping for third lunch. It must still be around the pole from second lunch stop! What a numpty! The bike came in the supermarket with me as I googled a cycle shop ahead for a replacement. I consoled myself with thinking of all the things I could leave behind the lock really wasn't a bad choice. The last 15 miles of the day were just horrible with the highway getting bigger and bigger until it was at least 4 carriages each way resembling the M25 around London Heathrow Airport. I hated everything about this and when I needed to go across 2 lanes for a junction, it was time to bail out. No chance of doing that manoeuvre and staying alive, so I jumped the barrier to re-route. The alternate road was also crazy with endless fast-food joints as far as the eye can see. I watched the miles slowly tick by, delighted when the time came to turn off into a lovely suburban road and find my hosts. They must have seen how exhausted I looked and went to town with looking after me. So glad for the uplifting company to end my second longest day at 112 miles, and my second and last night in Ohio.

DAY 33:
AKRON TO PITTSBURGH

A nother early morning after a late night happily chatting to my newfound friends and their unusual 'flying squirrel' pet! Having more of a heavy heart than ever, I left; with happy and priceless human interactions that filled my thoughts all day. I had picked up more people for my imaginary trailer, and took their spirit with me for a few hours, until the tiredness kicked in. The last three hosts were some of my favourite so far, and I knew, had I stayed in motels for those nights, I may well have been losing the will to live! Today I was heading for Pittsburgh, with a longer day than I wanted, but not much point in stopping 15 miles short of the city. No host tonight, so I had booked a place just over the river from where I would be coming in, so at least I didn't have to navigate a city. The two main advantages of no hosts were, a) I could turn up any time I liked and b) just crash out.

After 20 miles of being lost in my thoughts and very possibly asleep, I checked the map. I realised I had taken a wrong turn and diverted way too far north. My route memorising wasn't going to plan, and as before, annoyance was a bit of an understatement. Once I was up to speed I could keep going without too much discomfort. However, starting off was becoming very painful on my knees and undercarriage, with unnecessary stopping adding to both my physical and mental slog. I groaned every time I saw traffic lights ahead, and pretended I didn't know how the utterly stupid 4-way stops worked. Everyone seemed to wait for me at these anyway so I didn't bother slowing down anymore. The 'Stop, Speak, Smile and Sing' mantra from weeks before seemed like a patronising joke now, and detouring for nicer roads was also out the window.

Consequently, if the road looked long and straight on the map, that was the one for me, and I could claw some of these miles back by cycling the highway again the whole way. Getting to Pittsburgh and finishing leg three was the aim of the game today, with the icing on the cake knowing that I wouldn't need to go on road again for the rest of the trip. The re-purposed railroad and canal titled the 'Great Allegheny Passage' would take me through the Appalachian Mountains all the way to Washington D.C. This famous route (in the world of cycle touring anyway), connects a disused railroad and the 'Chesapeake and Ohio Canal' (known as the C&O) that span the 333 miles from Pittsburgh to Washington DC. Both surfaces are mainly gravel, which although not ideal, is heavily outweighed by beautiful scenery, no cars and the only flat route through the Mountains. Even if it took forever, it had to be a lovely way to finish, and the thought of it kept me going all day.

I finally rolled into Pittsburgh at 8pm after 111 miles with the sun setting behind the skyline. It was impressive with the expected 'industrial look' from its past mixed with modern skyscrapers and supersized bridges that tower over anything from the UK. There was no time for exploring and all I could think of was an early night. The end was now in sight and I was determined to enjoy the final few days.

DAY 34:
PITTSBURGH TO ROCKWOOD

'Here we go, bring on the cycle path' I thought, as I bombed it back over the bridge and out of the City. I did feel a little ashamed that I hadn't seen any of Pittsburgh, but I would remember the beautiful sunset over the skyline forever, and leave on a positive note. I felt that may not have been my lasting impression if I hung around too long! Whilst checking out the map and elevation the night before I wondered why I had planned such a big day. Over two and a half thousand feet of climbing on a gravel surface over 107 miles was going to be a tough day. Although the elevation was nothing compared to the other side of the country, I was just not use to it anymore. The only affordable place I could find to stay was a hostel 20 miles more then I wanted to go, and I needed to be there by 5pm! I was up against it, and there wasn't going to be much time for stopping today. I had picked up a map of the route, and it was comforting to see signposts counting down the mileage to

Washington, even if it was another 324 miles! This map helpfully indicated all the conveniences en route, and I reached my intended Breakfast café by 8am. My stomach was rumbling, but unfortunately it didn't open until 10.30am and there was no time for hanging about. I had reached the next by 10.00 to find 10.30 is just the time things open here. It was nearly 60 miles until I arrived in Connellsville for lunch, having eaten all my emergency protein bars. The only thing left was one sad looking energy gel that I had been carrying from the beginning. I would have to be desperate to 'eat' that yucky thing, and I think I just put it in my pack as that's what 'proper cyclists' do!

After some much needed food, I stopped counting the miles down and started to appreciate this lovely route. It was the sort of place you would come out for a day trip, and I was definitely out of place slaloming around the happy families and day riders. I greeted everyone and had some lovely chats along the way with anyone who wanted to engage. I had some fun with some younger male cyclists who passed me as I stopped to buy an ice-cream. I quickly overtook them with my friendly 'hello' whilst licking a Mr Whippy ice-cream (with added flake of course). I had two thoughts about getting this on video to amuse my friends, but one hand off the bike was already cocky enough!

Later on in the afternoon the joy faded as I ran out of energy realising there was no way I was going to make the hostel by 5pm. The long slow miles had caught up with me and I completely 'hit the wall' and sat down on the nearest bench. There was only one thing for it, it was time to get the energy gel out. Maybe the sugar or placebo effect would trick me into getting back on the bike? It was totally grim and I made a decision to NEVER eat one ever again, it was worse than being hungry!

10 slow miles later I cycled up to the lifeless and closed hostel. To my surprise there was a note on the door with my name saying I needed to come to a restaurant further up the road. With relief that they had thought of me I apologised many times about my tardiness to the lady in the restaurant. She was so nice and said she had been worried about me all day on my own and had called, text and emailed me. I don't know who she had been calling or emailing but it wasn't me! I thanked her for her kindness (not letting on that I had not received any of these communications) as I felt bad enough already. It turned out that I had reached the restaurant just in time. It was the only place to eat in the town and was closing in half an hour. I was so hungry having only one proper meal in the 107 miles, and said 'Whatever you have, I'll take it!'. I ended up with a USA sized burger and chips, and all was well in the world again. I had completed my last century day, and looked forward to crossing the 'Eastern Continental Divide' in the morning for a downhill run to the finish line. There was no way I wouldn't make it now; I was nearly there.

DAY 35:
ROCKWOOD TO PAW PAW

I was a bit of a wreck this morning, having been abruptly woken up every couple of hours with the horns of the passing trains. As sleepy as I was, it was always easy to get going in the morning when breakfast is a town away. After food, it was up and over the divide with some gorgeous views and a history lesson about the Mason-Dixie line that historically passed through this route. This demarcation line (or political and geographical boarder) was used as the divide between the Northern 'free' states, and the Southern 'slave' states during colonial times. The history between the West and East of the USA could not be any more opposed in my opinion, and can be easily seen in the ethos, ideologies and political stances of the two sections. It's easy to see how 'uniting' this country and all its States is a near impossible job. Which state you live in defines so much about the lifestyle, economy and political views of its residents.

It was lovely to be cycling alongside so many trains today, something that has been a constant throughout the trip always making me smile. There were no borders between the cycle track and the rails, I could have easily walked along the tracks like they do in the movies. This 'Alleghany Passage' came to an end just over the border into Maryland in the cute town of Cumberland. With a quick lunch stop and a continued history lesson around the route museum, I headed straight out onto the next part, switching to the 'C&O' canal towpath. The hopeful continuation of positivity didn't last long with this new track a world away from the fine gravel of the former. The unloved rocky towpath was a shock to the system, definitely not the surface for my bike. Having not anticipated this, there was no pre-prepped route alternative, and much faffing occurred every couple of miles for possible road alternatives. With the canal carving its way through the mountains, trapped between a train track and a river, it couldn't be avoided altogether. It was a 'my way or the highway' moment, and reading how steep the climbs were in travel blogs, roads seemed a mad option when there was a flat alternative. I would just have to put up with the bone shaking ride for the next couple of days and hope it got better.

The 30 miles to the final stop of Paw Paw did nothing for my saddle sores, and I was pleased and slightly bemused to arrive in the very small town. Some of my previous hosts said, 'You'll know when you are in West Virginia', and I now knew what they meant. I had crossed the river from Maryland and the difference was clear. Nothing awful, just a surprising difference to the more 'up market' tourist vibe I had been cycling through. Not to be confused with Virginia, West Virginia is continuously ranked as one of the poorest states in the USA, cut off geographically by the mountains to its richer neighbouring States.

The accommodation was far cheaper and the 'Bike Path' hostel was easy to find. It wasn't really a hostel, just the house of a cycling enthusiast who let people stay in his spare rooms. It was anything from fancy, but he was very welcoming and all essentials were covered. The second room was also being occupied by a cycling couple who evidentially weren't up for socialising, so I made my way to the local restaurant in a house three doors up. It suited the town's vibe with the fried food options written on a whiteboard, with a relaxed 'everyone knows everyone' ambiance. I happily didn't get any questions tonight, as I wasn't in the mood and was trying to be inconspicuous. I felt my only non-cycling top was made for this occasion blending in with a plethora of checked shirts. I just needed a straw hat and a beard and I would have nailed it. I was in 'Hillbilly' country, as described by every outsider, and didn't realise the change would be so sudden by just crossing a river. How little I had learnt from entering the mid-west reservations and the suburbs of Chicago as to how the culture could change from one mile to the next. Wikipedia describes the term 'Hillbilly' as "*a term (often derogatory) for people who dwell in rural, mountainous areas in the United States, primarily in southern Appalachia.*" The stereotype depicts shotguns, floppy hats, banjos, and bad teeth etc. I was happy and unsurprised as always to find normal polite people just going about their daily business. I was well use to being warned about the 'next town' constantly on my trip and didn't take much notice anymore. People were people wherever I went, and had encountered no problems or reasons to be cautious. Although being a complete outsider from a different country and blind to local politics, would only help my opinion in this case. I killed some time in the evening sitting on a park bench swigging apple juice from the carton and devouring the most disappointing chocolate raisins ever. 'Proper chocolate' was definitely on the 'wait till I get home list' along with cheese and tea. 'Not much of a wait anymore' I said to myself, one and a half days more rattling on this track and I'm done, how hard could that be?

DAY 36:
PAW PAW TO HARPERS FERRY

t was nice to have breakfast cooked for me early in the morning, whilst learning more about the local area. The owner had moved here as he really loved cycling the track and earned a living by hosting passing cyclists. Now, when I say 'he loved it', I mean, I've never met anyone so enthusiastic about cycling the same canal towpath every day and checking in on the wildlife. I wished I could be as content with life as he seemed to be, cycling the same track each day. Maybe one day I will make it to this stage and stop wondering what's around the next corner. Although I wasn't sad to leave this town, I was glad of my local knowledge I was now armed with. My host had informed me of a brand-new bike track being constructed parallel to the tow path. It had not been connected up from this direction, but I had specific instructions on how to locate it.

These were,

> ➤ After mile marker 144 look left for an overhanging tree with some flowers at the base, and a piece of rope on the opposite bank.

> ➤ Keep your eyes peeled, it's not obvious and you'll cycle straight past if not actively looking!

> ➤ Once located, follow the small muddy path into the trees for a couple of minutes until as if by magic a brand-new cycle path will appear!

It all sounded very suspicious, but with no doubt I shot out of town early on my new mission. Before mile marker 144 my spirits were kept high by deer darting across the track ahead and passing through the famous Paw Paw tunnel. An 1850 engineering marvel for its day, cutting straight through 950 metres of mountain. It looked truly ancient with no visible updates, not even a light inside. I thought about locating my bike lights, but somehow thought that would be cheating and cycled into the pitch black with my heart in my mouth. I followed the dripping sounds ahead, only bashing into the wall and the rail a few times before fixating on the light at the end of the tunnel. If this had been in the UK it would definitely require lighting, a 'proper' surface, up to date handrails, a hard [inset space] hat, obligatory safety briefing, and with plenty of 'don't sue us' signage, completely ruining the experience. I just loved finding all these strange things along my travels where you take responsibility for yourself and get a choice in living life!

Counting down the mile markers, some beautiful scenery, and a wave to the odd camper distracted me from the surface. I found some bonus fun along the way trying to get the ancient water pumps working. One actually did and I filled my bottle with some suspiciously coloured water that would need to be replaced asap! I finally made the 144 mile marker just as my host had said; I saw the tell-tale piece of rope and a small track. After a few minutes pushing my bike the brand new immaculately tarmacked bike path appeared. It was like a beautiful mirage and a very odd thing to see in this oldie worldie place. Like the "room of requirement" in Harry Potter, it was just what my bum and achy arms needed as I sped along happily to the next town where unfortunately the magic cycle lane ran out.

In the afternoon I was back on the track trying to zone out and distract myself with music, when suddenly the bike's front wheel locked up. The next thing I knew I was on the ground gasping to breathe with the bike on top of me. It was one of those moments when a million things go through your head in an instant. 'Is this the end of the trip?', 'That's surely the end of my bike?' and 'I had come so close to fail now' were the main three thoughts running through my head. Funny how these came above any possible injuries! After moving all my limbs and pushing the bike off me, I cautiously got up to my feet and was over the moon that I hadn't broken and bones. I then noticed a lady shouting 'you went straight over the bars and landed on your head!' She had seen the whole thing and was figuring out how to get me to hospital. It was half nice having someone there, and half embarrassing at the same time. I think the adrenaline was running through me.

Although I had a gash on my knee, along with cuts, scrapes and was clearly winded from the bike hitting me, I was delighted I had gotten away with it. In fact, I was elated and was laughing off my embarrassment while my new friend was shouting 'your helmet saved you, I'm going out tomorrow and buy a helmet!' Whilst I was glad that I had convinced someone that helmets were a good idea, I figured she wasn't a bike mechanic or going to be massively helpful in this situation. I located some plasters in my bag and tended to my leg, then gathered my belongings scattered over the track including my headphones, which were still playing music from a nearby bush. The adrenaline was now wearing off and I removed my helmet to find it had a crack in the side, which would likely account for some slightly blurry vision and pain in my shoulder. I would figure that out when I was somewhere more useful than this track in the middle of nowhere.

Whilst my new friend was doing an excellent job of fending of questions from passing cyclists, by shouting 'always wear helmets' at them with the odd 'Hallelujah' here and there, I tended to the bike. A piece of tree branch lodged between the wheel and the front fork, answering the question as to why the wheel completely locked up. No amount of pulling and pocking was moving it, but after 10 minutes of stabbing it with my bike tool it broke up. To my absolute astonishment the wheel spun true with not even a tiny buckle. I couldn't believe my luck, someone up above was definitely looking out for me today. I was fine, as was the bike, so therefore time to crack on. I thought I should tell someone back home about the incident, especially as I had fallen on my head, so I could be kept an eye on from afar and accountable for my actions. Or more truthfully, not be told off at a later date! However, it seemed I was in the only spot on my trip so far with no phone signal! What were the chances of that? I decided to wave goodbye to 'shouting lady' thanking her for her 'help' and reluctantly pootled the 10 miles to the next town, looking out for random stray branches.

It was the slowest cycle of the trip so far and the longest 10 miles to a café for a massive break. I'd managed to send a message home along the way, and a few friends were looking up medical centres, bike shops and generally being super supportive. They even managed to find the correct 'Williamsport' I was heading too, as I often forgot how many towns with the same names there are in the US! It was suggested I head to the café that I was already in as they had spare bike parts. I hadn't even seen the mini cycle section in the corner before reading the message and did a quick look around the room to see if my friend was actually here spying on me! I clearly should have off loaded some of my route planning to this lot, they were amazing, and isn't technology just brill when it works! This info was great, however all I really wanted, of course, was a cuddle, which I very much hope won't be replaced by technology, but the love through the phone was super and cheered me right up. I promised to tell the server that I had hit my head (which was a very bizarre exchange), and she said I could stay as long as I liked. No free drinks here though, I should have timed my accident for Nebraska!

After a time, my blurred vision eased up and there seemed no point in sitting about much longer. Even though the obvious thing was to get back on the towpath, I had a complete mental barrier to it now, and decided I would take the road. The tarmac was lovely, but obvious why no one cycles the roadway through these hills. The gradients were nearly impossible to manage, and I stayed in 1st gear most of the way either climbing or freewheeling. I wouldn't recommend it, and was glad it was only 25 miles into the historic town of Harpers Ferry, and to my host.

A chilled evening and an appreciative stay, although much more functional than the up-beat happy families I was getting far to use to. My hug would have to wait to another day, and I pitched for an early night. I only had 65 miles to push myself and the bike through tomorrow, then I could properly relax. I couldn't decide if I was more excited for the impending finish line achievement, or just to finish and get off the bike. Either way I was happy. I was arriving in Washington DC ahead of schedule, and could use my contingency for sightseeing, sleeping and whatever I liked. So pleased my bike got through unscathed today, a walk to the finish with a broken bike would have been a very sad ending.

DAY 37:
HARPERS FERRY TO WASHINGTON DC

There was no particular need to be up early today, but I just wanted to get going and was out the door at dawn. I planned to take my time and slow plod the last 65 miles to Washington. Luckily, a slow plod was all that I was going to manage when combining the tow path with my stiff legs and shoulder. I had trouble lifting my arm above my head but keeping it in bike position was not a problem. As I knew I was going to make it today, I mentally switched off and found it hard to focus on anything apart from the distance. I literally counted down the miles the whole way, which is not a fun place to be in, especially as the route got busy and I was constantly stuck behind people traffic. The USA do not have many bank holidays each year but today of all days happened to be 'labour day' and the world had come out to play! There were a few sights along the route I was planning to see, but the huge crowds put me off, and I slowly carried on weaving my way down the path. Usually, I would transfer to the road, but having to navigate my way in seemed like way too much mental effort today, I was definitely in plod to the finish mode!

Eventually in the early afternoon, the canal turned into a river and deposited me right into the city centre. I was hoping the Lincoln memorial would be easy to find, and gladly it was - no problem at all. Like everything in this country it was massive and not at all subtle, instantly cheering me up as I went as fast as possible around the people obstacles to the finish line. Cycling all the way to the base was evidently not possible on this National holiday. It had been a long time since I had seen so many people, and my thoughts of carrying the bike up the steps for a photo finish wouldn't be happening today. Instead, I half hid the bike in a random bush and ran up the steps mentally shouting 'get out of my way'. Far too polite to actually shout this, I comically fought my way through the crowds to the top greeting Abraham Lincoln and having a solo dance party much to the amusement of the crowd who couldn't get away from me quick enough. Not exactly the end I have imagined for weeks but it will have to do! I had wondered how I'd feel at the finish line. Would it be one of those life affirming moments of fulfilment and pride? Or perhaps crying with pain and exhaustion? In reality, it was just too busy for any major dramatics, and after the ten second celebration, I stood there not knowing what to do with myself looking like a very sweaty fool! I eventually rescued my bike from the bush and brought it halfway up to the oversized terraces, and finally sat down. It was all a bit of an anti-climax with no one there to share it with, but some very happy video calls to friends followed, and I was a happy girl. It really was a beautiful place, looking out over the reflection pool to the Washington Monument, with a sense of calm and relief. I sat there for about an hour with a happy contented grin on my face, thinking about where I had started 3335 miles away in what seemed like a different world. I had achieved more than I thought I would be able to cope with, and couldn't remember the last time I felt happier within myself and with the world. Although the details, time frame, and stats that kept me going definitely ticked the 'achieve' box, it was the people I had met and the sights I had seen which filled my head and would do for months to come. Often to me our world seems increasingly divided, helped along by the news and social media where 'news' generally equals 'bad news'. Although I may have been looking through my rose-tinted cycle shades, at this moment in time I could not have loved humanity more. Definitely something that travel always has the power to do, taking me out of my comfort zone and dropping me into the unknown. If I wasn't before I left, I had truly been bitten by the cycle touring bug and had already made loose plans for future trips.

Over the next few days, I daydreamed about new adventures as this trip sunk in, whilst racing around being a tourist, and foraging for packing materials for the bike. The discomfort in my knees and from the fall seemed heightened now, but nothing was going to stop my 'go go go' regime in a hurry. I was mentally wired and on a complete high and hoped that this feeling of fulfilment would last forever. I was literally starting work the day after I got back and couldn't wait to jump back into life and hatch new plans for my next adventure whatever that may be!

EPILOGUE

ast forward nearly 3 years later to spring 2022, and I am still writing this book! The whole world has been on its own crazy adventure of living in a pandemic with extreme life restrictions. Following an energetic return to work in the Autumn of 2019, a truly fantastic year topped off with a bonus adventure examining in India, we all literally stopped overnight in March 2020. It's now 2022 and I think I have blanked out most of the last 2 years. You would have thought with all that extra time on my hands I could have written several books! Indeed, I should have, but the thought of looking at the computer screen after a day of Zoom lessons, constant rearranging and generally being sad, writing a book about happy things that I could not do… I was left with little inspiration.

I got there in the end, and even though I could tell you little about what I did during the pandemic, I can still recall every day and all the details of my trip. The non-travel time makes the experience ever more prominent to me and I am even more grateful that I went the year I did. I still constantly daydream about the time, knowing that it has helped me in so many ways, on top of just being a lovely memory.

Going on my own was definitely something that made me stronger, opening up conversations that being in a group simply doesn't allow. I would recommend this to anyone, and especially with modern technology, as my experiences were all shared back home in real time. If this technology was not available to me, I think I would have struggled far more than I did with loneliness and keeping a positive attitude. Having said that, sharing this experience with someone would have been brilliant too and I won't rule out having a cycle buddy in the future.

I remember thinking that as I didn't cry at any point in the trip, I could have pushed myself more with increased mileage in the first week, finishing in a faster time. In my 'never satisfied but always content' outlook this does make me smile now. I'll always want to push myself more, but maybe I already missed so much by going faster? Also, my knees have not 100% recovered and finding my 'breaking point' sounds like a crappy trip ending! For me, having the necessary time restraint kept me going and was a positive goal, but I could have easily lingered around these places more and had an altogether different experience. As much as I'd like, I'm never going to break any world records for speed, and there's no point in cycling through somewhere and having no experience of it. A definite balancing act for future trips when wanting to see as much as possible in the time available.

One thing I will be repeating for sure, is the bike and the gear, or more precisely, lack of gear. The bike packing system worked well and not really having any stuff was both liberating and effective. This was important for me to cope with the mileage whilst enjoying my ride. The only thing I have made a mental note to take next time is an electric toothbrush, maybe a pair of sandals, and another t-shirt wouldn't go amiss! Having said this, does the bike or the gear really matter for an adventure? I know this is something that puts people off all the time, not having the 'right' stuff. I would say to anyone that was thinking of going on a trip even for one night, if you have a bike and a backpack you are all set. You can learn everything else as you go, and don't let the expense and 'advice' of cyclists and retailers telling you what you 'must have' put you off. I would say, you must have a sense of adventure and a 'can do' attitude, everything else is optional. The choice of gear will make the trip easier, more convenient and hopefully more enjoyable. I certainly spend less time fixing my bike at the side of the road than I use to, and am generally more comfortable than on past trips.

However an adventure unfolds and whether it goes to plan or not, the unexpected things, funny moments and beautiful sights are the things that last forever in my mind. In short, all the things not planned or practised. I hope now as the world has mostly opened up again, that it hasn't changed in spirit and is as welcoming as it was. I can't wait to get back out there again and see for myself on my ever-increasing adventure list!

And there you have it. Thank you so much for making it all the way to the end of my little story and rambling thoughts. I hope it has made you smile and helped bring this part of the world to life. I wish you all well in your own adventures and hope to have you along with me on another one soon.

APPENDIX

DAY	CYCLE DAY	MILAGE (MILES)	FROM	TO	ELEVATION (FT)	STATE
1		4	London	Seattle	550	Washington
2	1	59	Seattle	Arlington	1200	Washington
3	2	56	Arlington	Marblemount	800	Washington
4	3	87	Marblemount	Windthrop	7500	Washington
5	4	50	Windthrop	Omak	2150	Washington
6	5	65	Omak	Republic	4318	Washington
7	6	56	Republic	Arden	4250	Washington
8	7	90	Arden	Sandpoint	2700	Idaho
9	8	90	Sandpoint	Thompson Falls	2100	Montana
10	9	105	Thompson Falls	Missoula	2500	Montana
11			Day Off			Montana
12	10	85	Missoula	Lincoln	2650	Montana
13	11	91	Lincoln	Townsend	2800	Montana
14	12	108	Townsend	Livingstone	1660	Montana
15	13	88	Livingstone	Joliet	1900	Montana
16	14	85	Joliet	Hardin	2400	Montana
17	15	95	Hardin	Sheridan	1300	Wyoming
18	16	111	Sheridan	Gillette	2674	Wyoming
19	17	76	Gillette	Newcastle	3470	Wyoming

DAY	CYCLE DAY	MILAGE (MILES)	FROM	TO	ELEVATION (FT)	STATE
20	18	94	Newcastle	Rapid City	7000	South Dakota
21	19	98	Rapid City	Interior	3300	South Dakota
22	20	133	Interior	Valentine	4000	Nebraska
23	21	112	Valentine	O'Neill	1900	Nebraska
24	22	78	O'Neill	Norfolk	430	Nebraska
25	23	102	Norfolk	Omaha	150	Nebraska
26	24	100	Omaha	Winterset	2900	Iowa
27	25	100	Winterset	Sigourney	550	Iowa
28	26	103	Sigourney	Davenport	2200	Iowa
29	27	104	Davenport	Ottawa	1400	Illinois
30	28	92	Ottawa	Chicago	800	Illinois
31			Day Off			Illinois
32			Day Off			Illinois
33	29	103	Chicago	South Bend	515	Indiana
34	30	70	South Bend	Angola	358	Indiana
35	31	93	Angola	Pemberville	125	Ohio
36	32	112	Pemberville	Akron	472	Ohio
37	33	111	Akron	Pittsburgh	1400	Pennsylvania
38	34	107	Pittsburgh	Rockwood	2648	Pennsylvania
39	35	75	Rockwood	Paw Paw	1000	West Virginia
40	36	82	Paw Paw	Harpers Ferry	2700	Mary Land
41	37	65	Harpers Ferry	Washington	614	District of Columbia
42			Day Off			
43			Day Off			
44		**3,335**	Fly Home		**81,384**	

Printed in Great Britain
by Amazon

83247953R00095